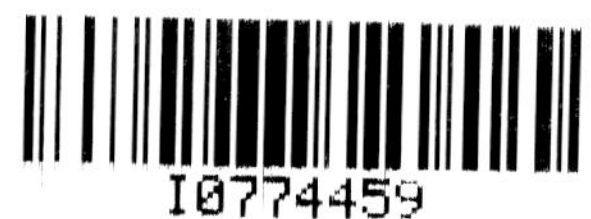

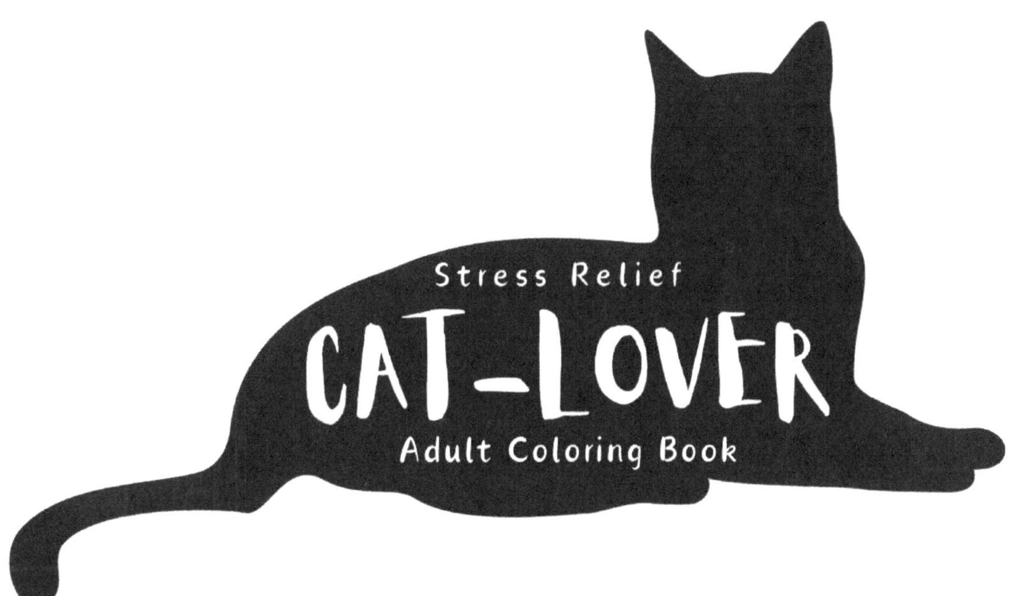

For Esteban and Karina.

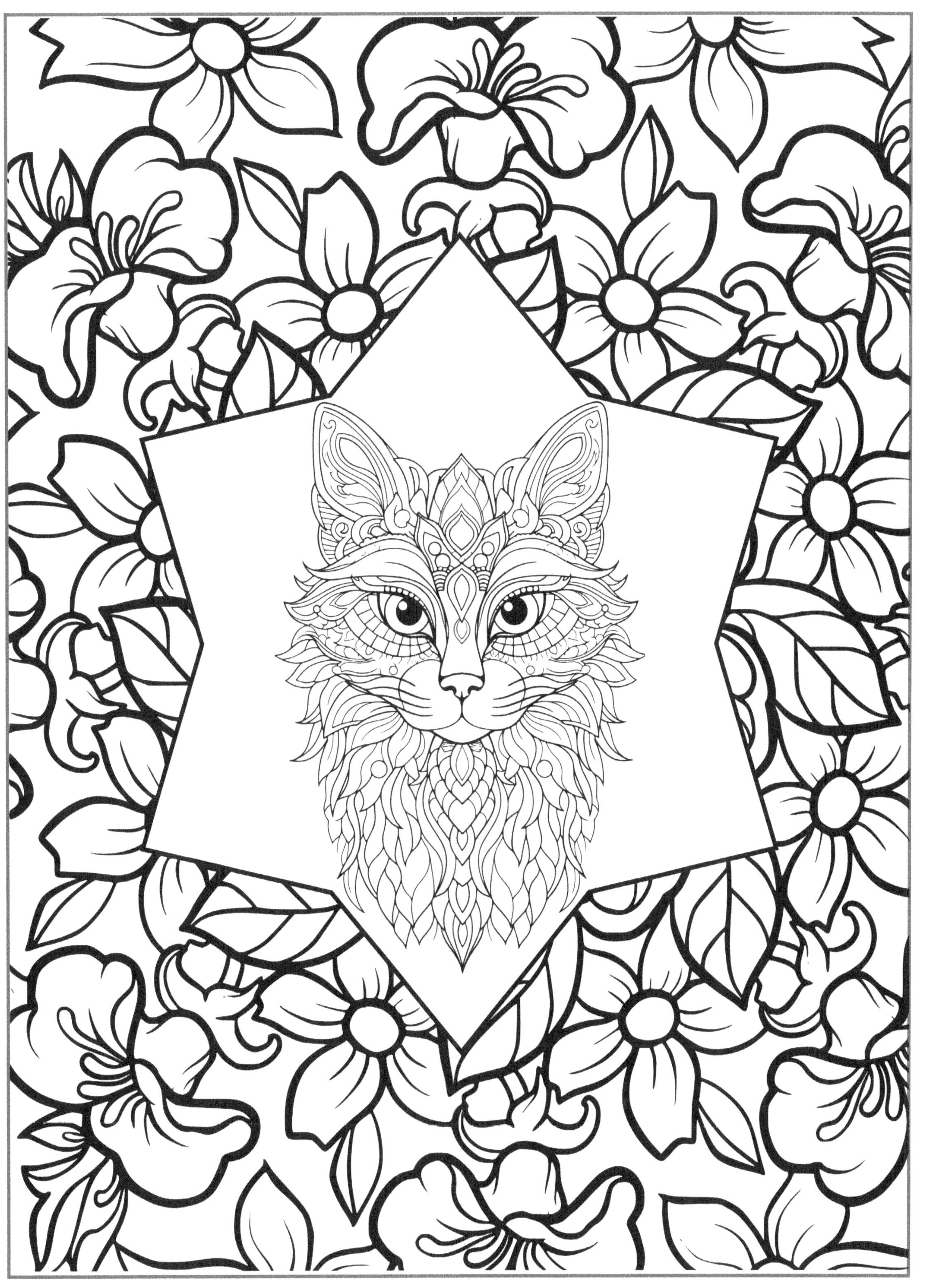

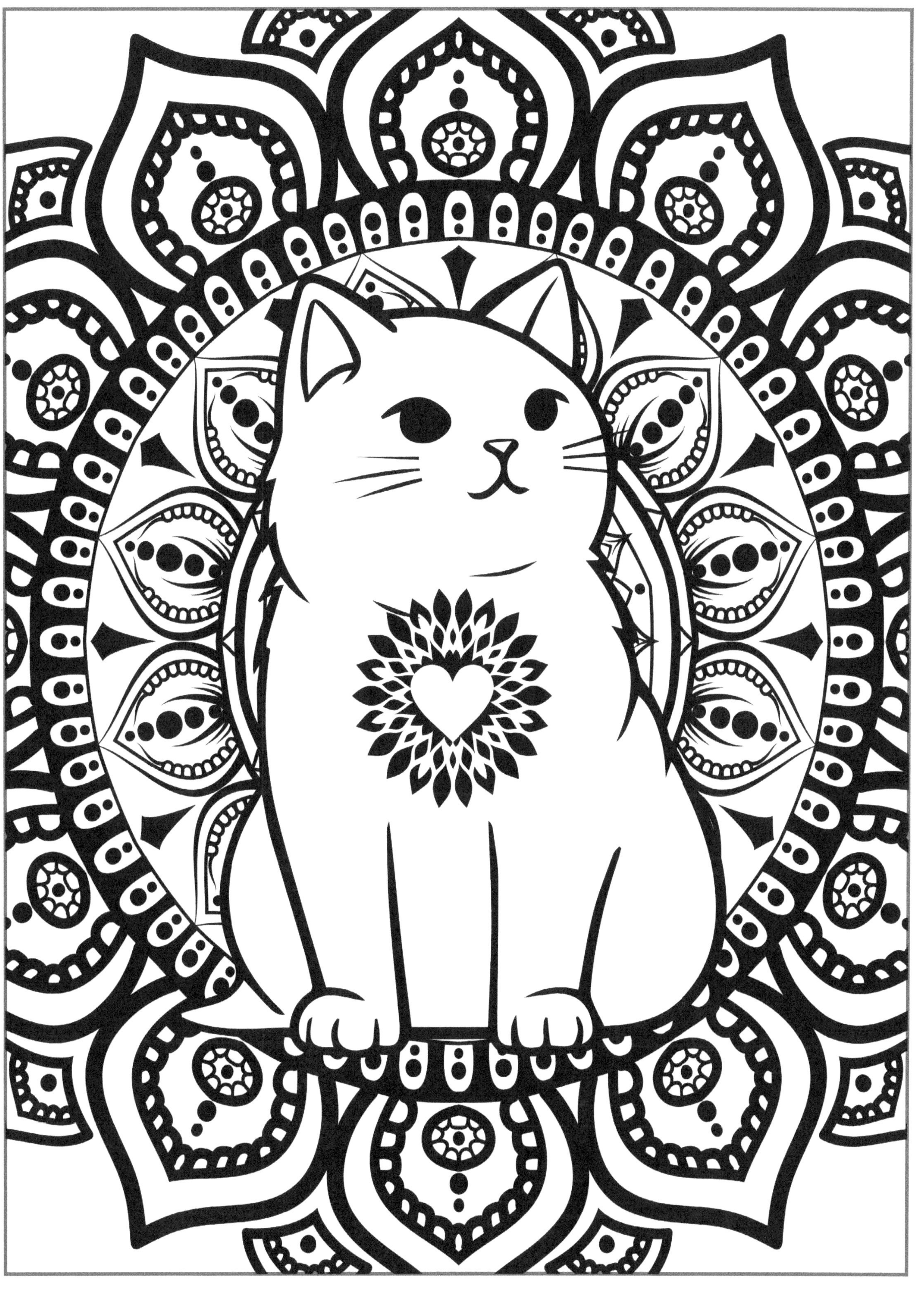

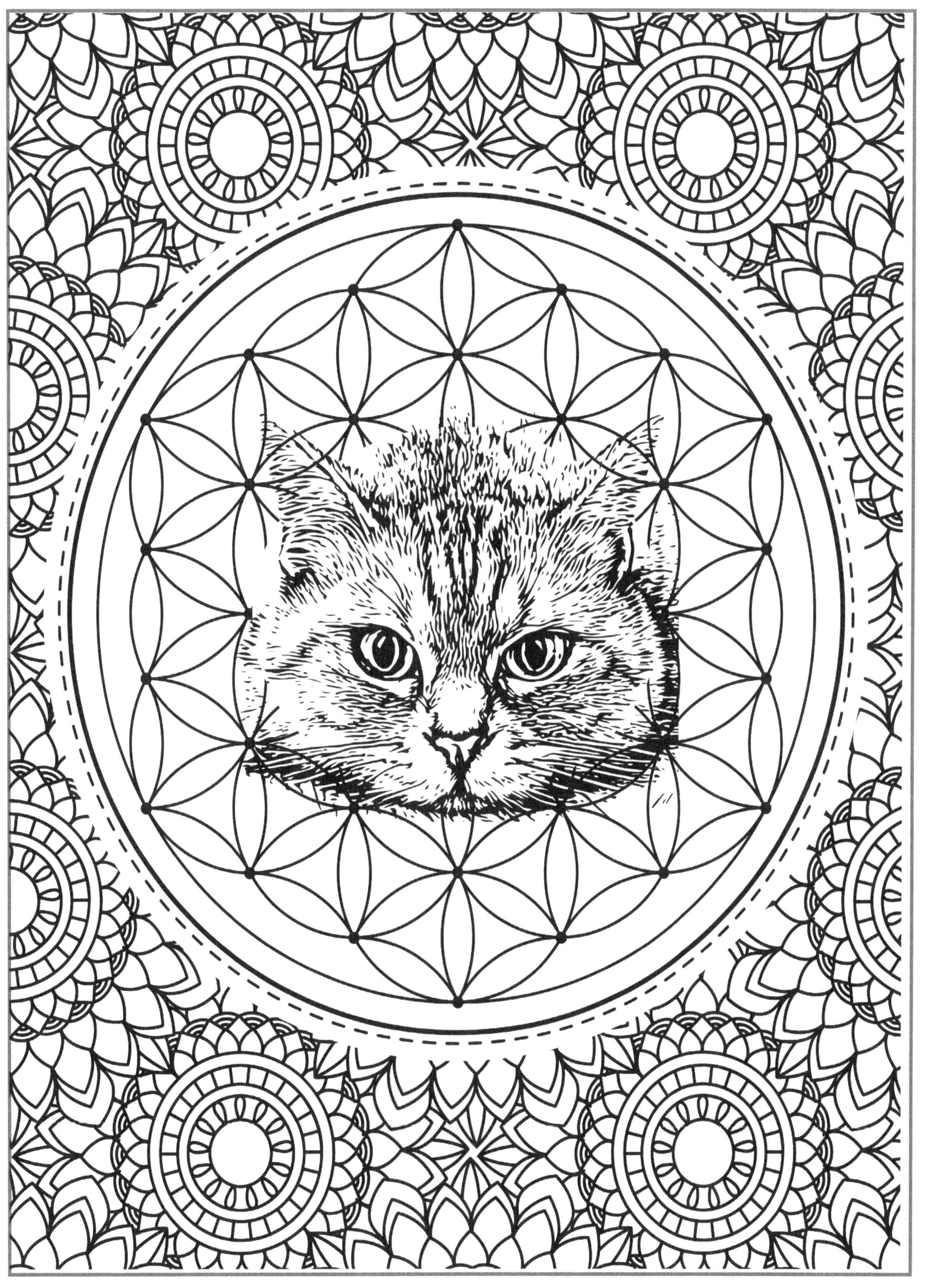

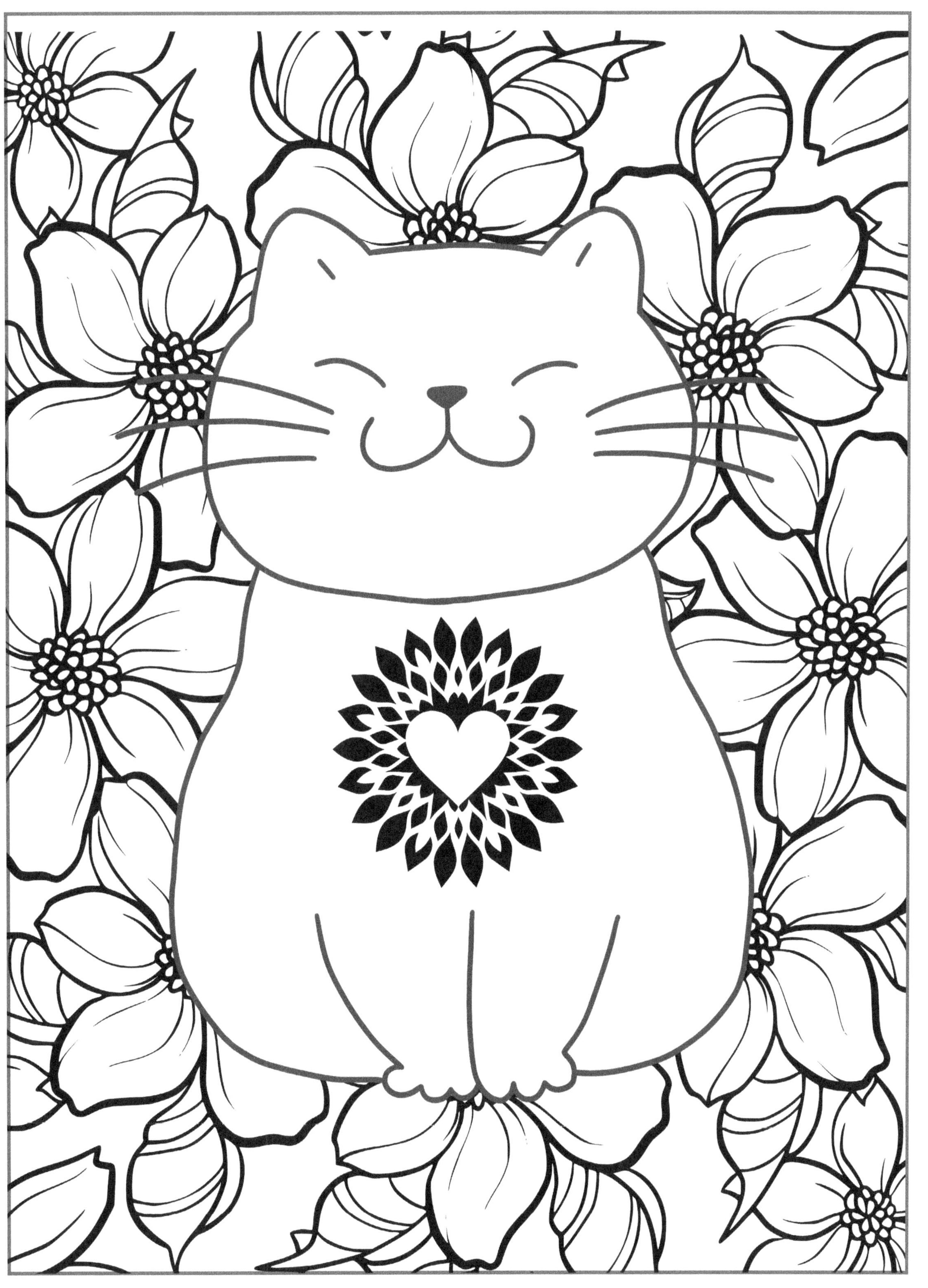

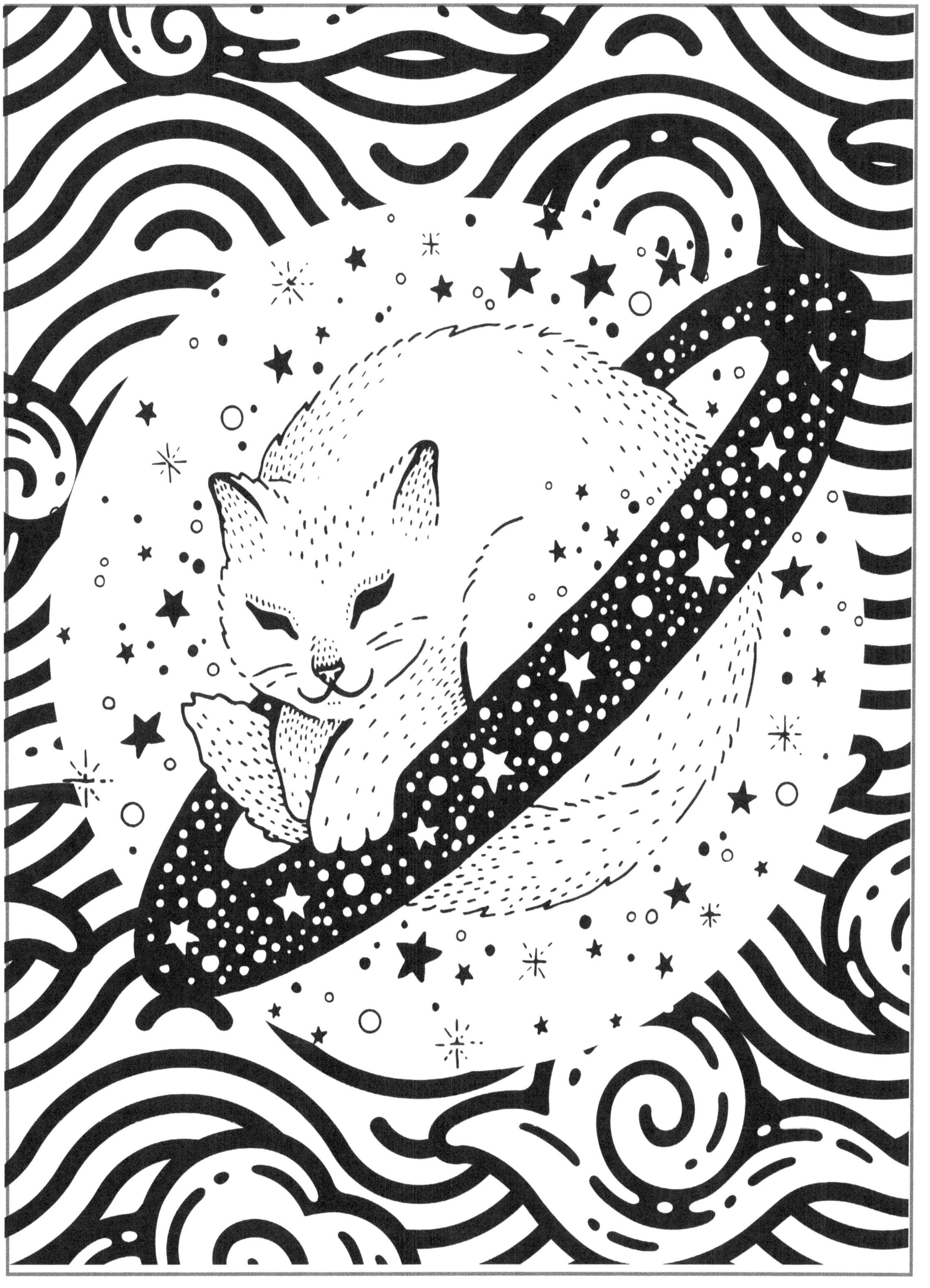

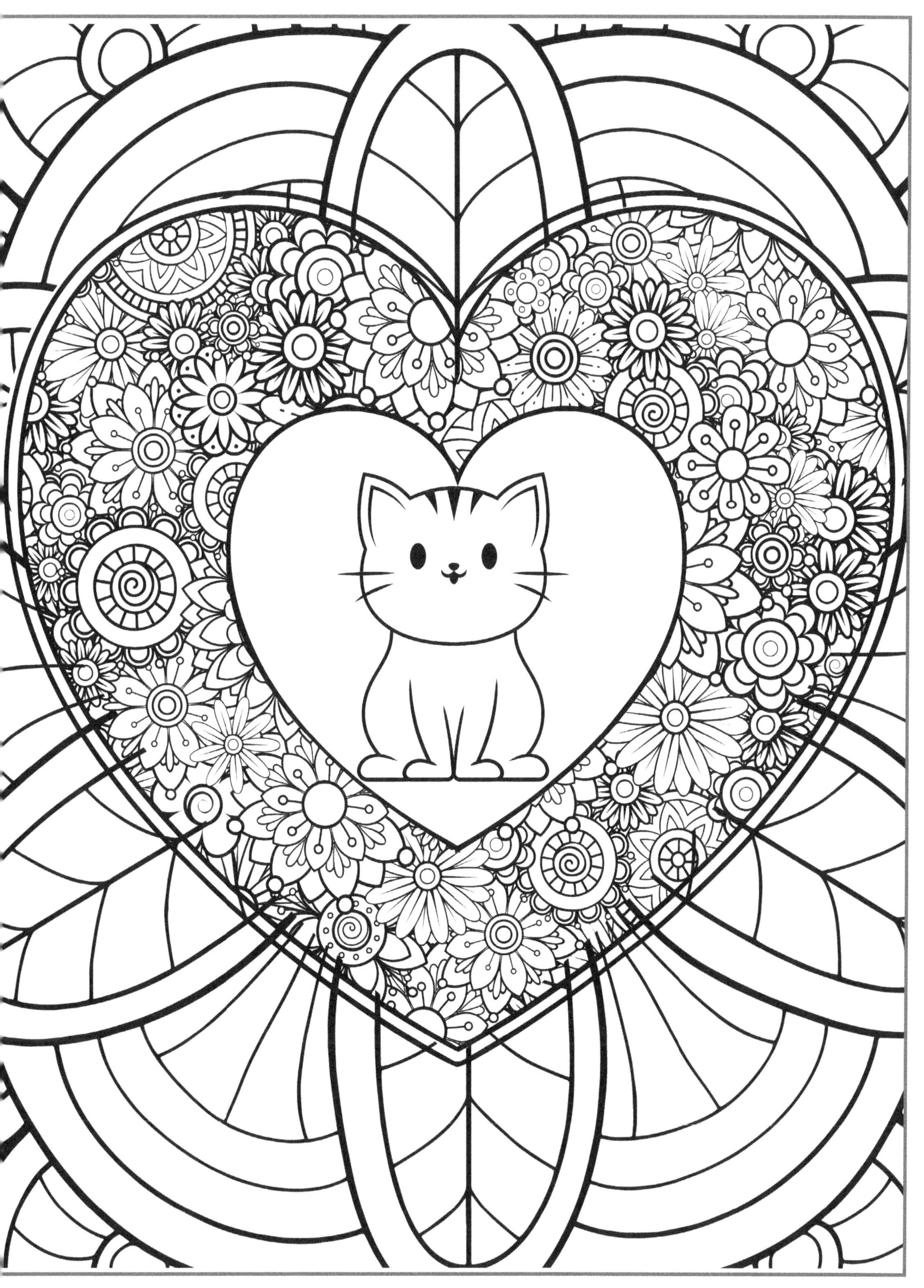

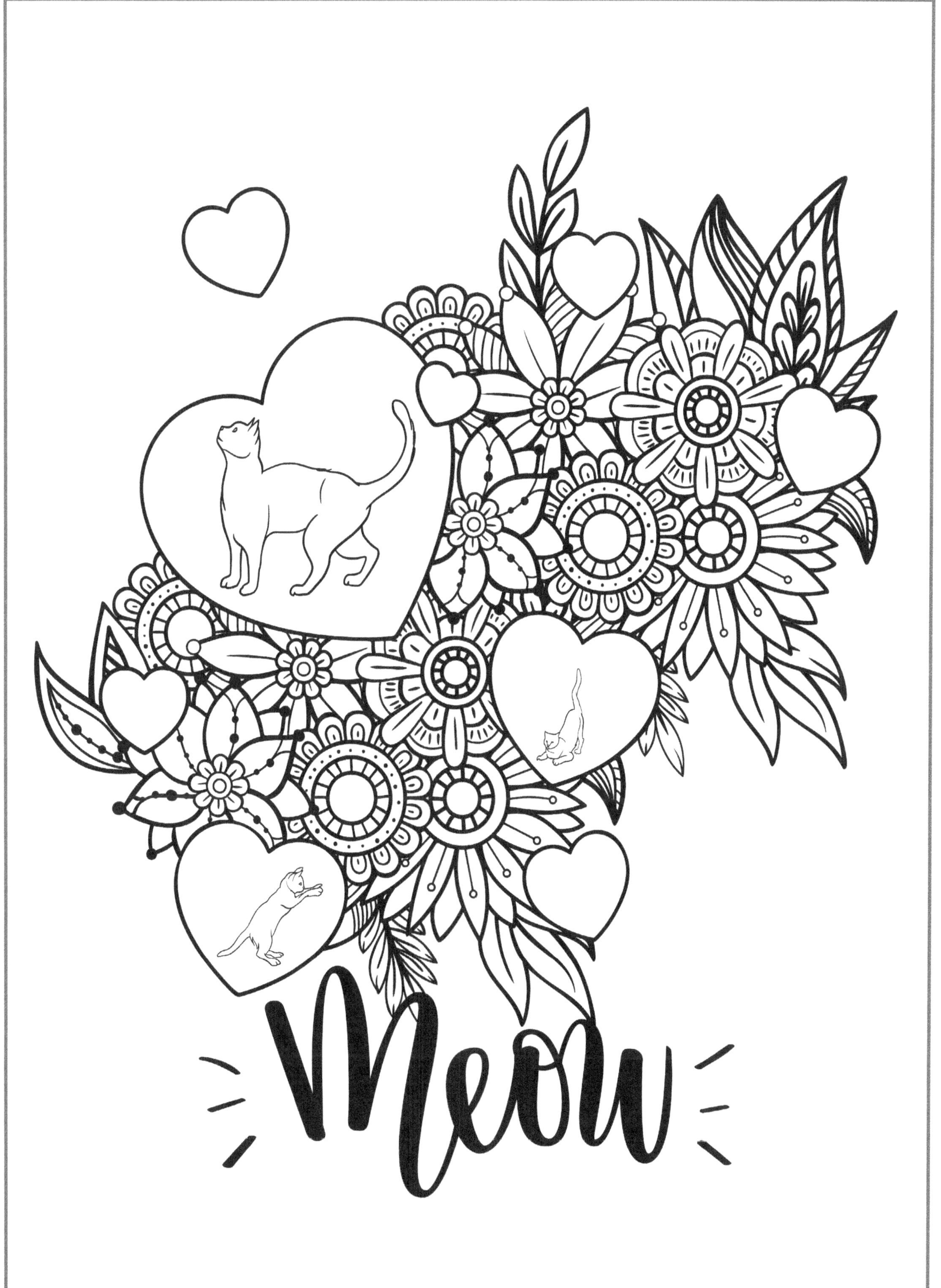
Meow

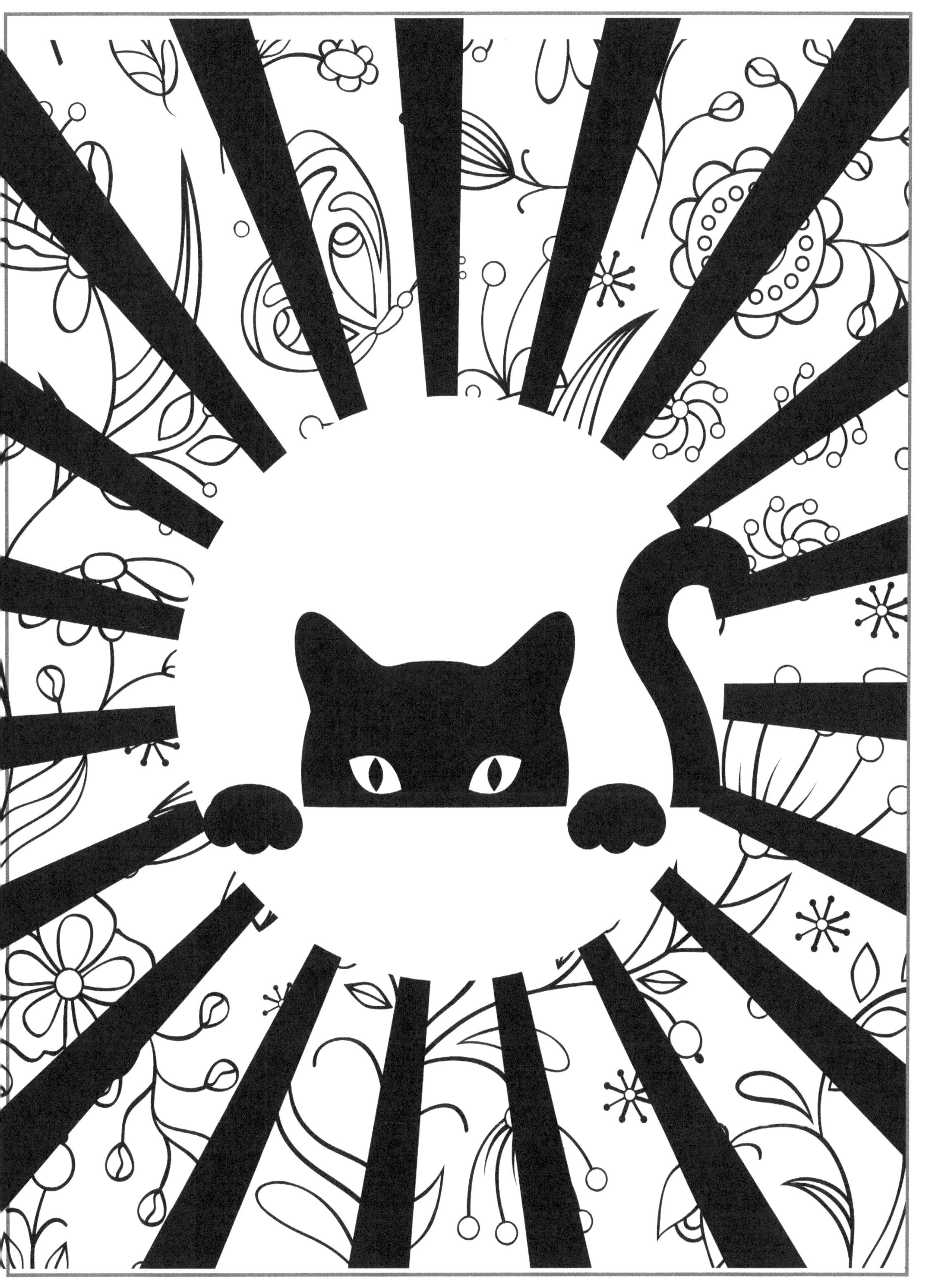

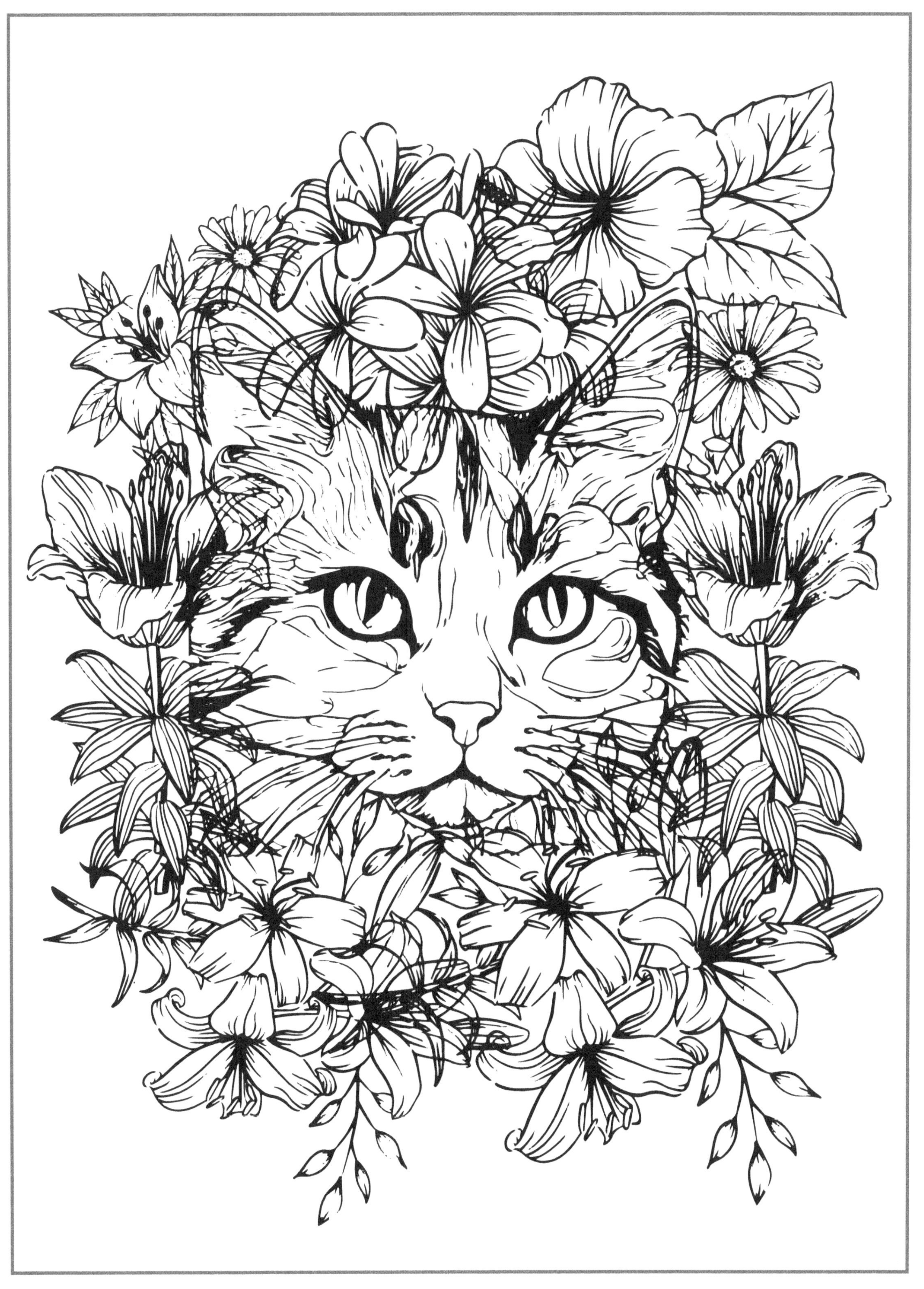

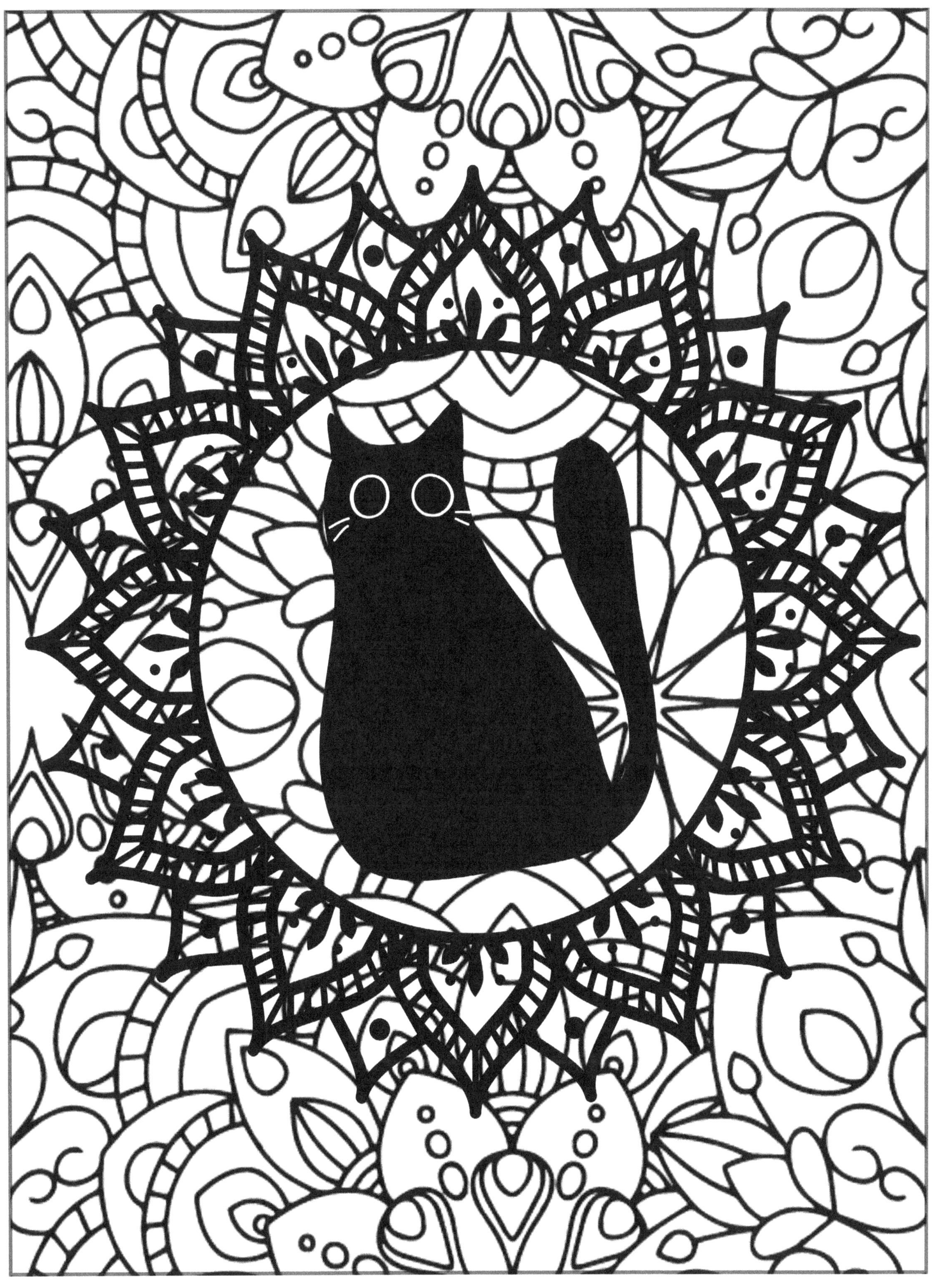

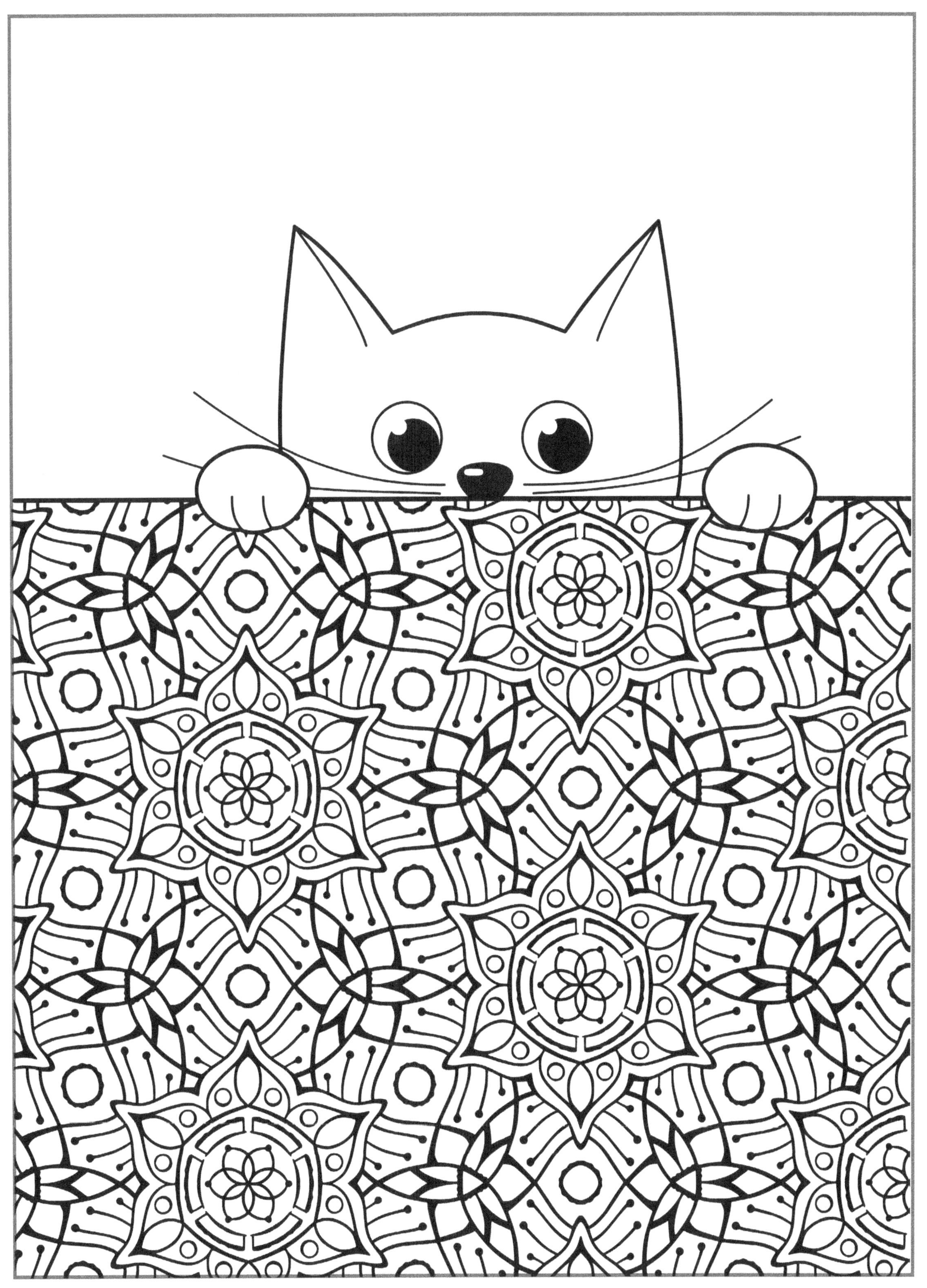

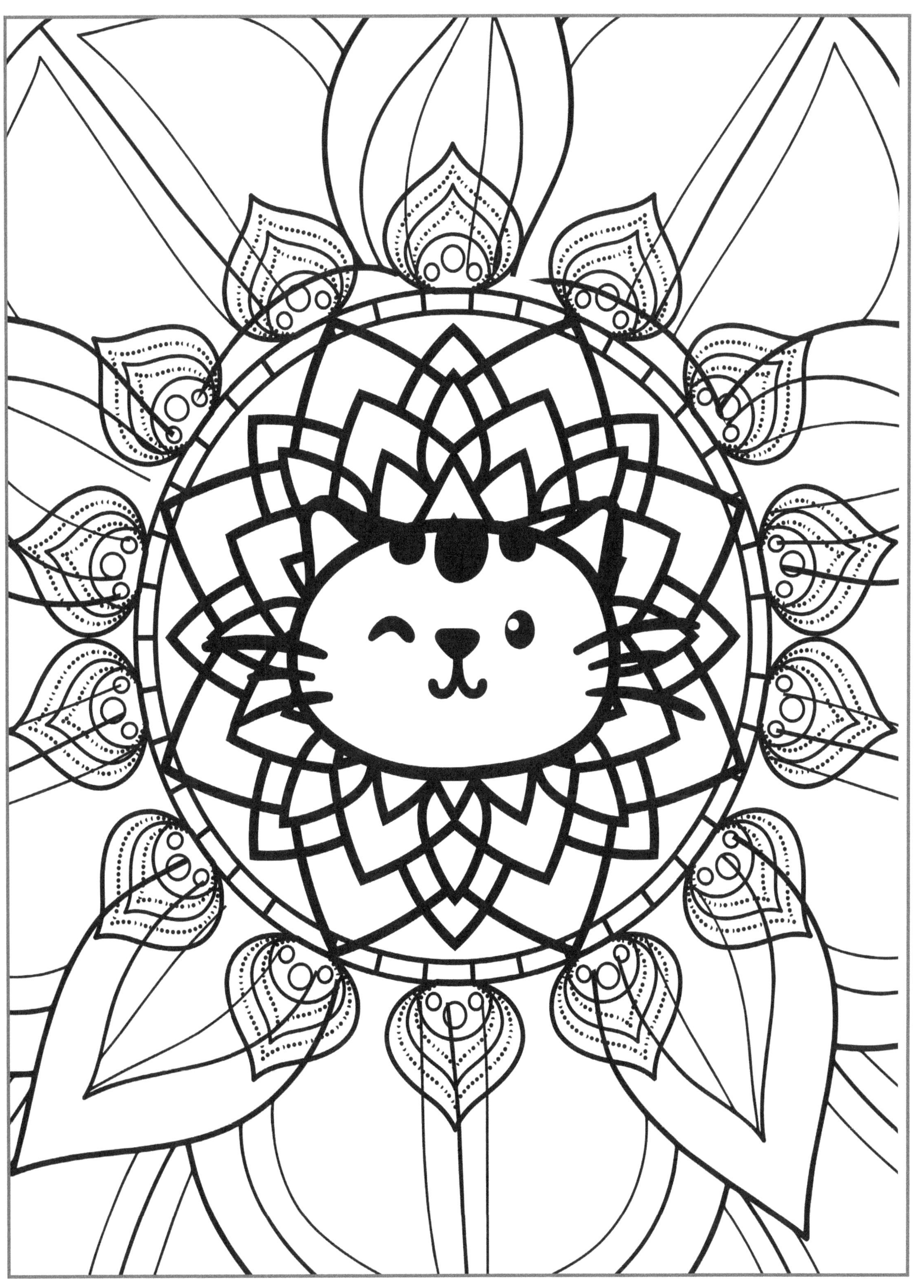

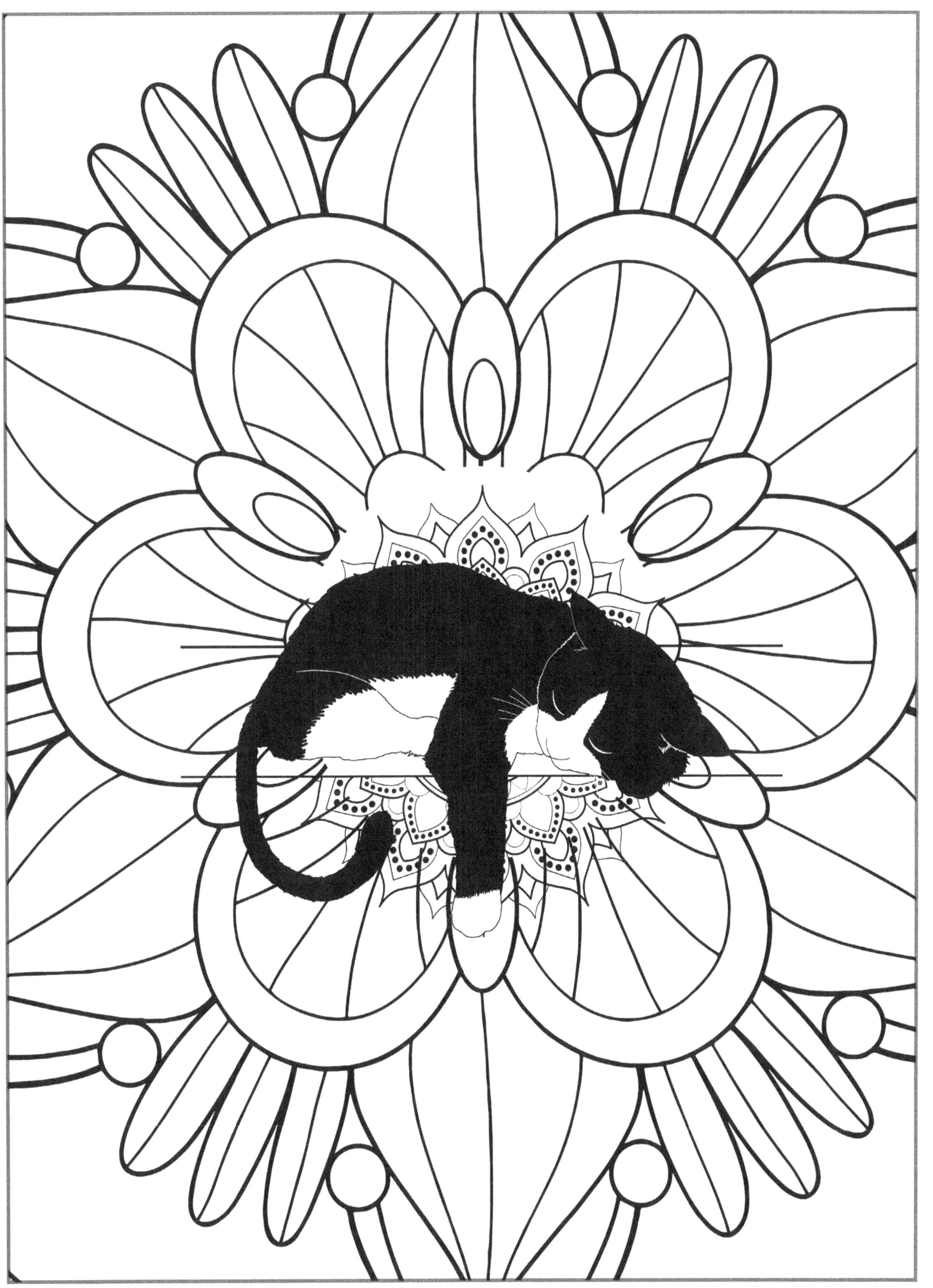

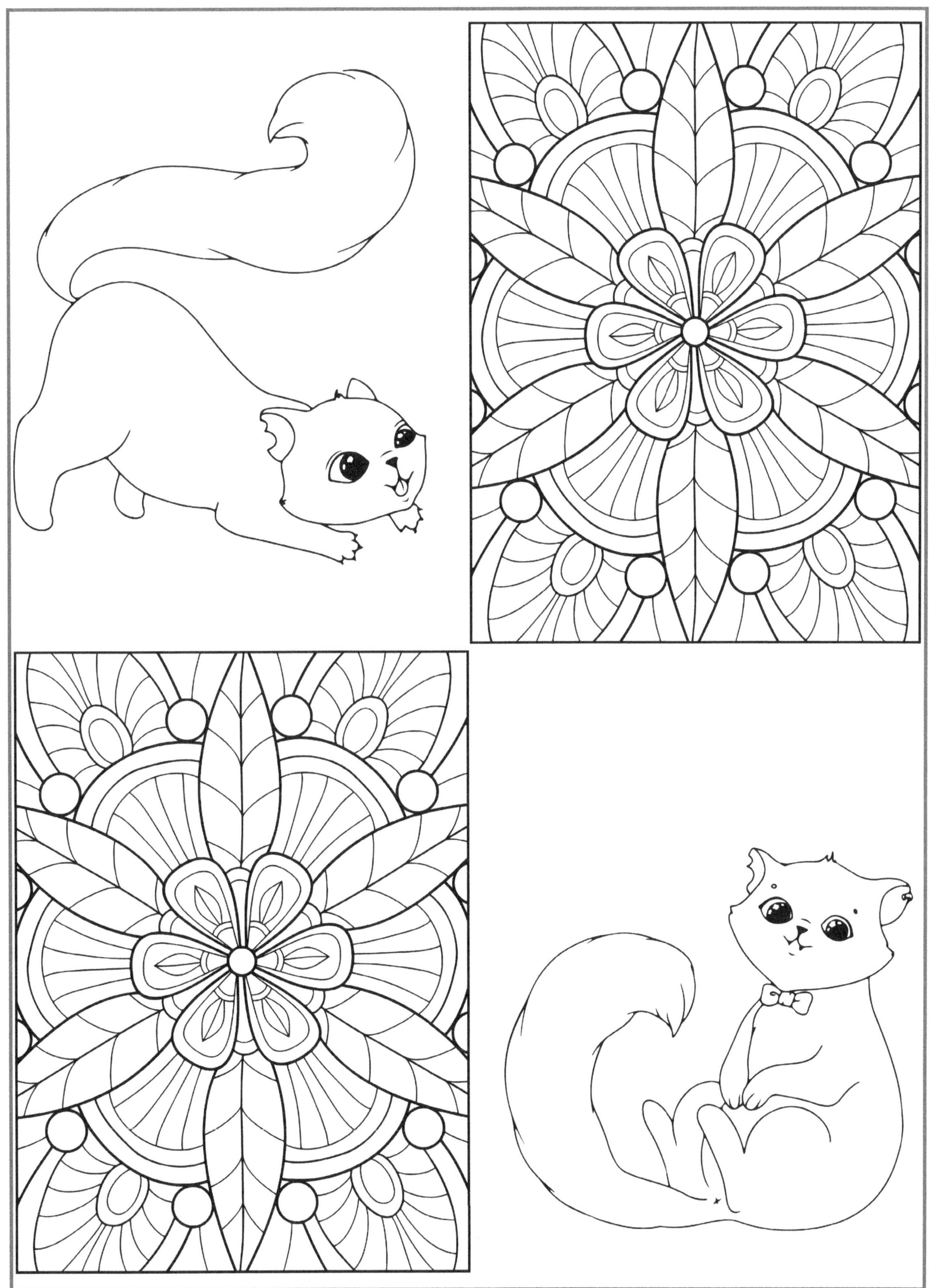

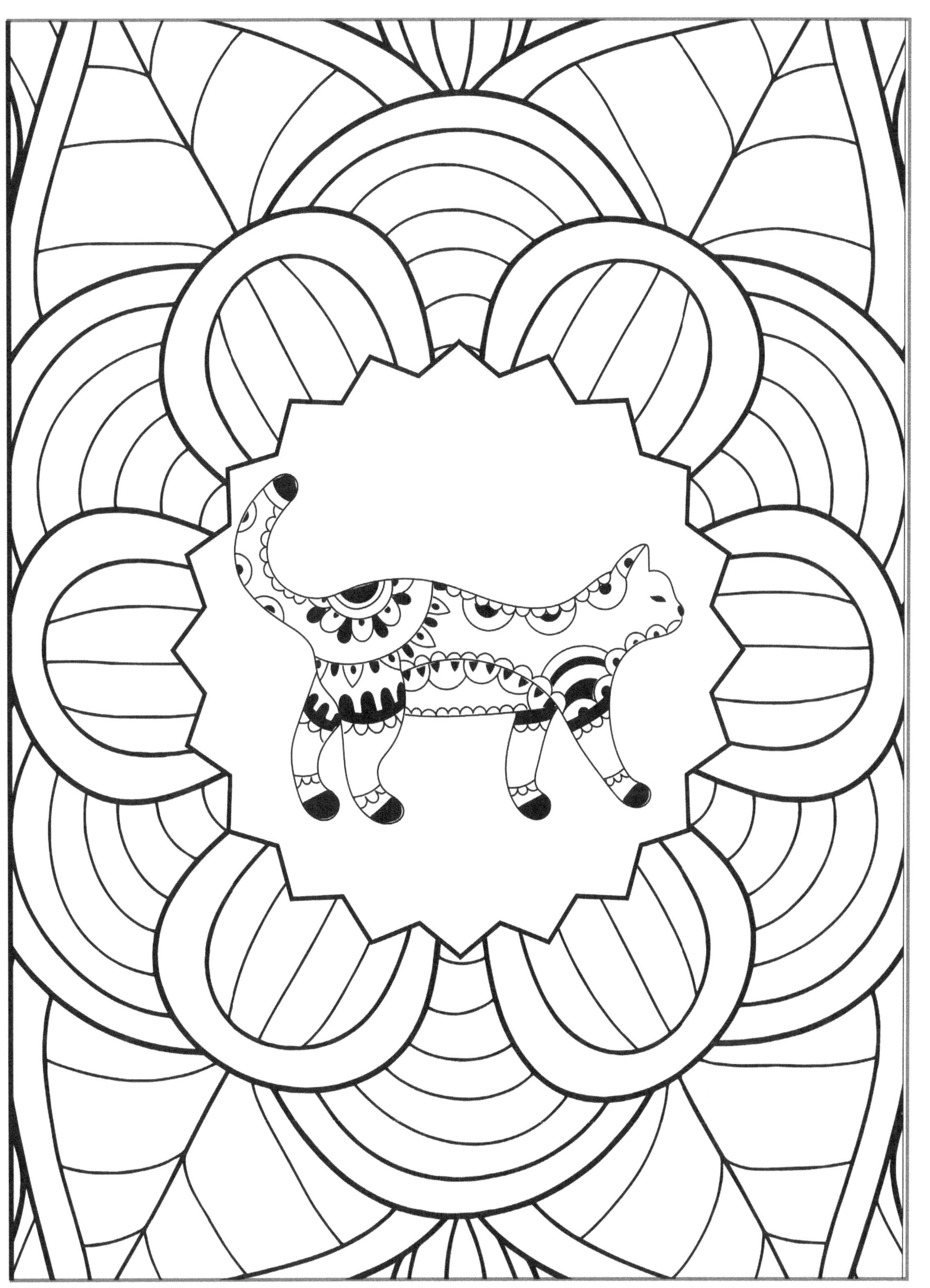

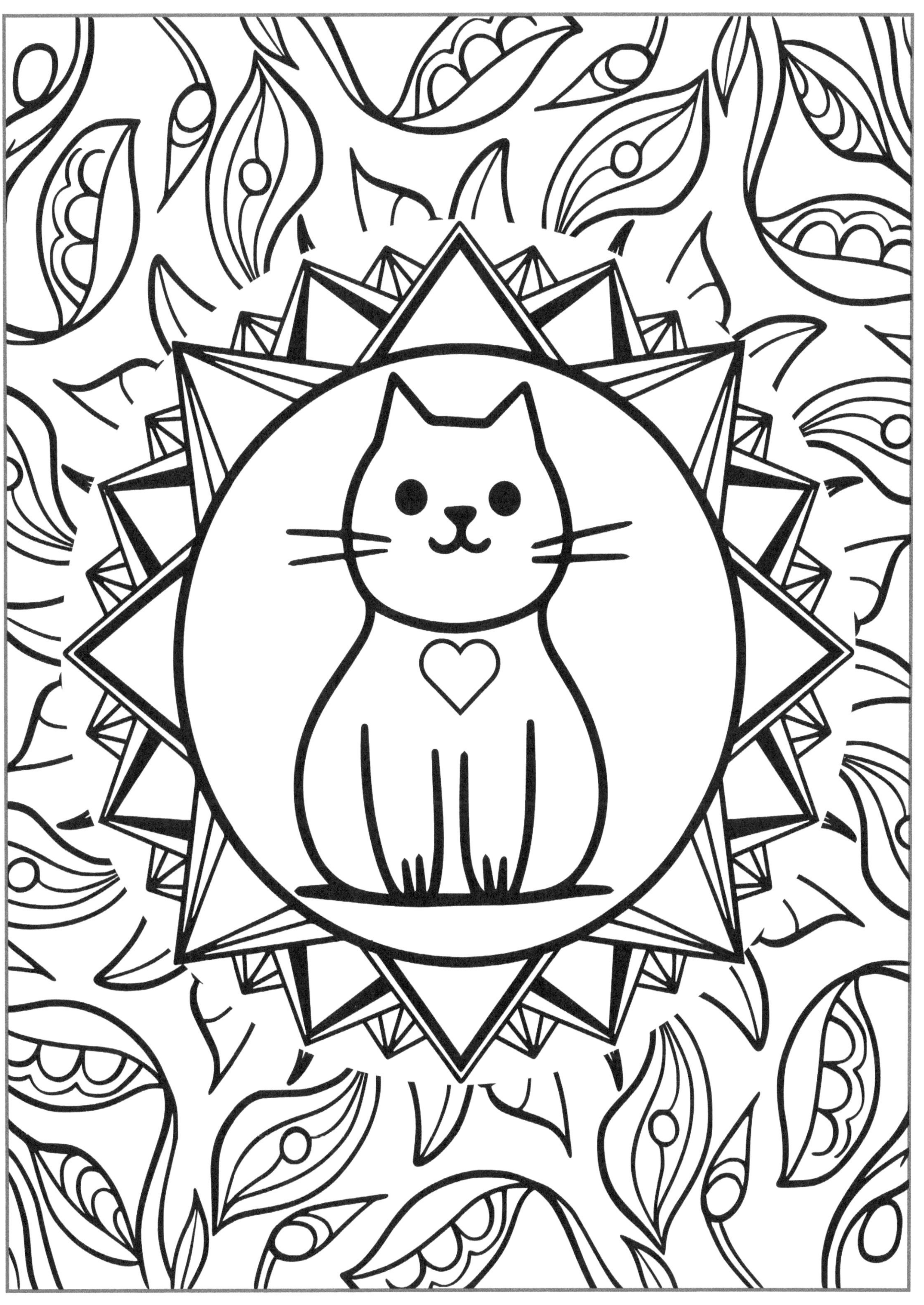

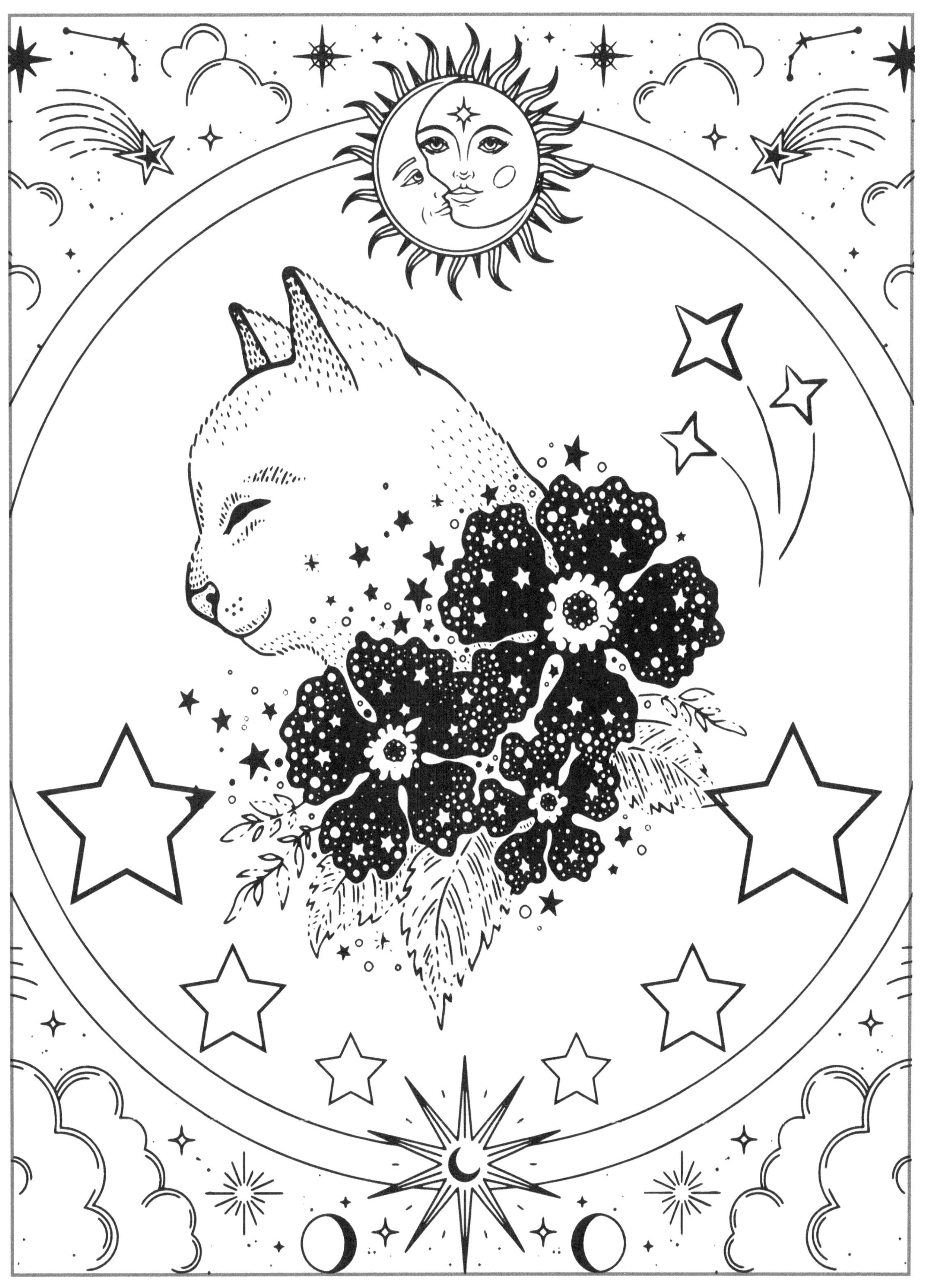

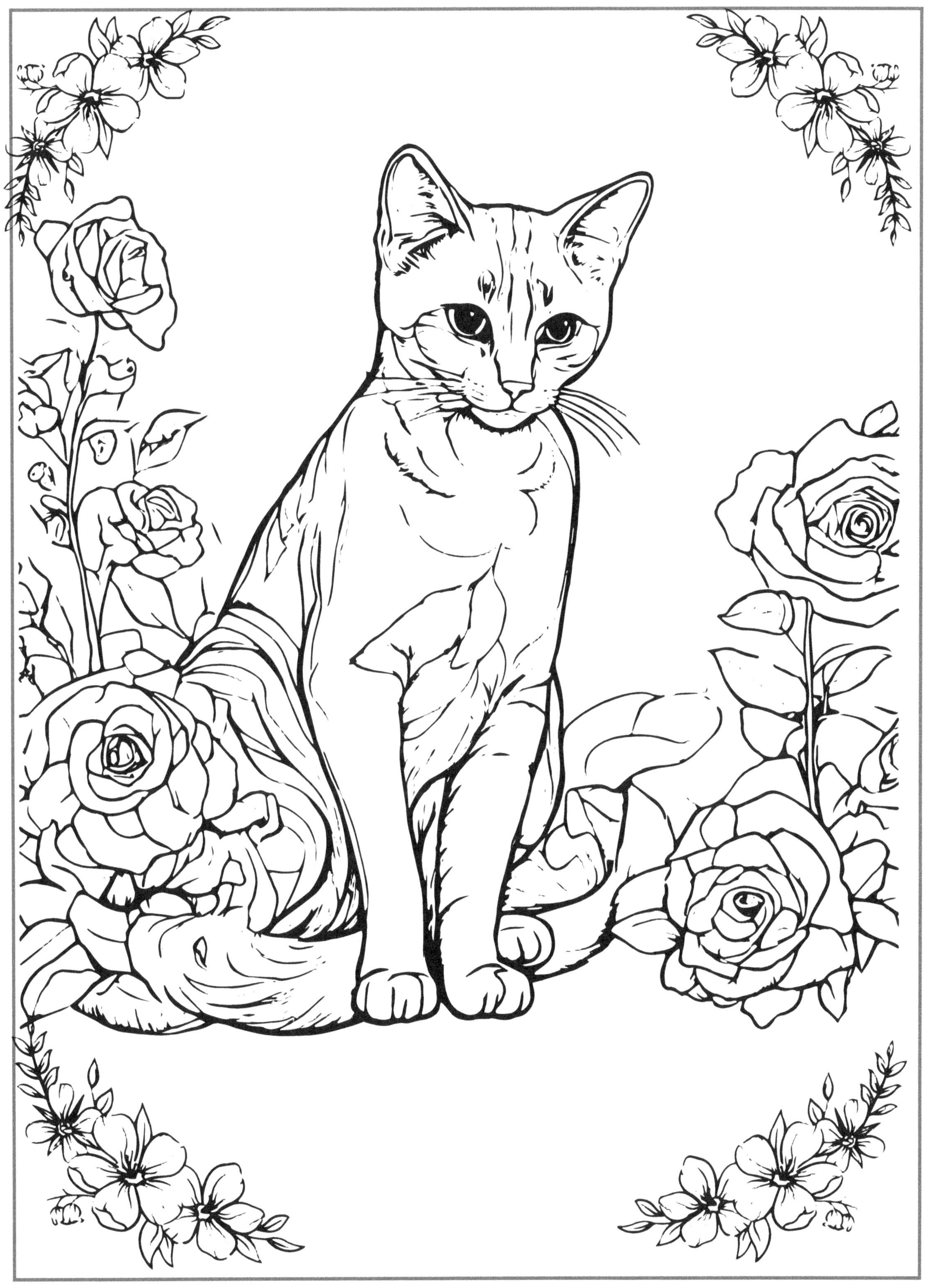

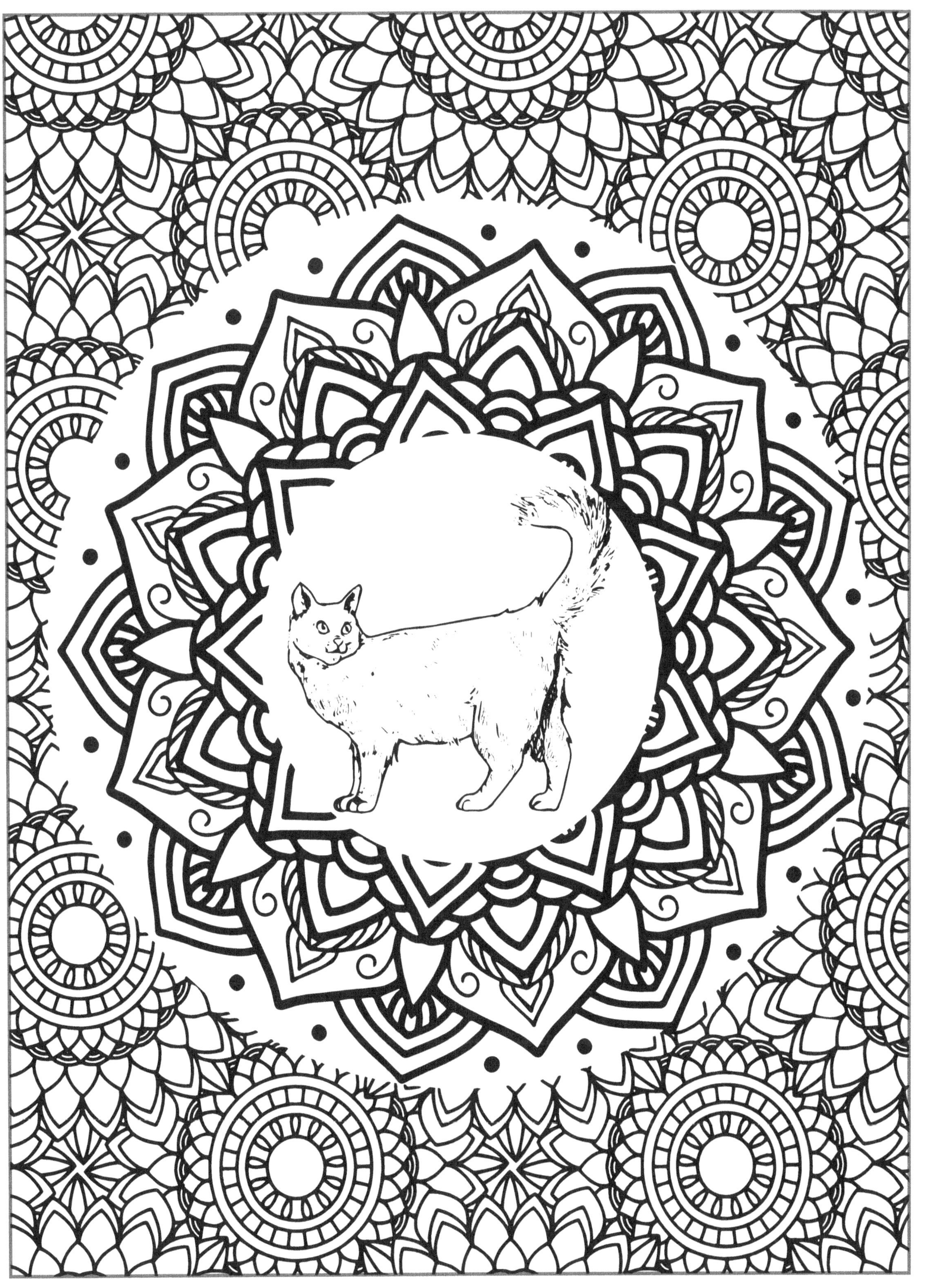

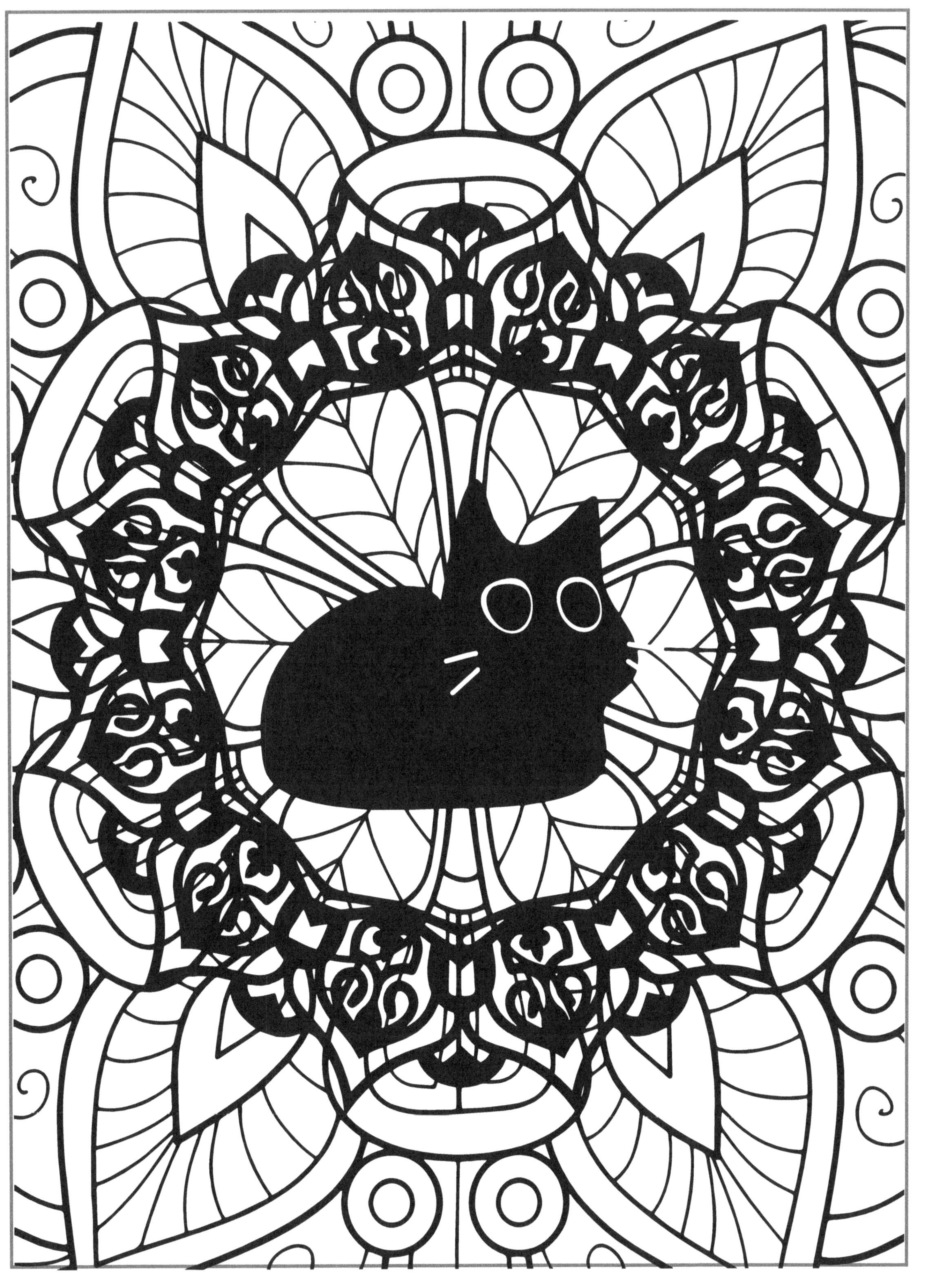

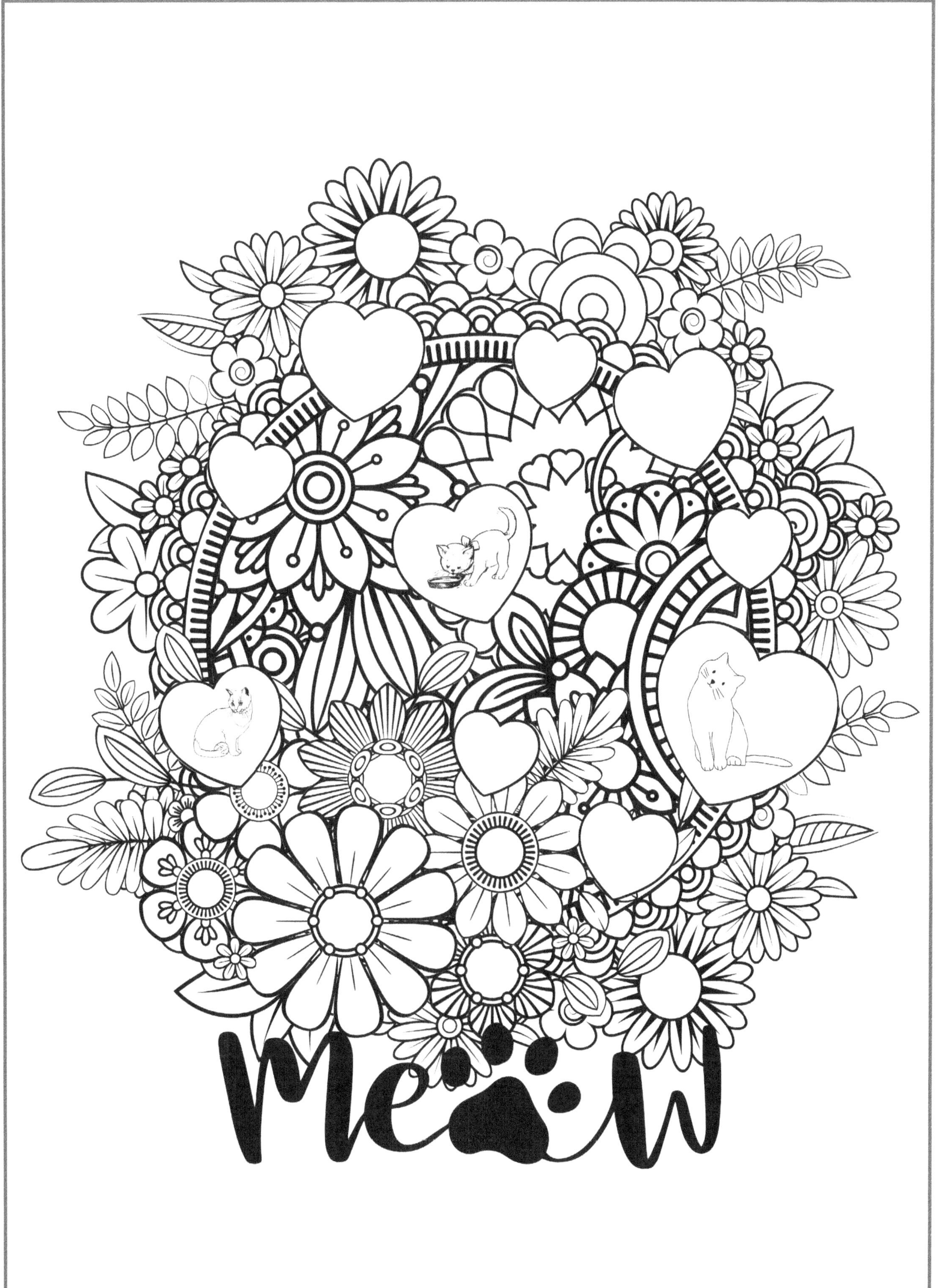

MEOW

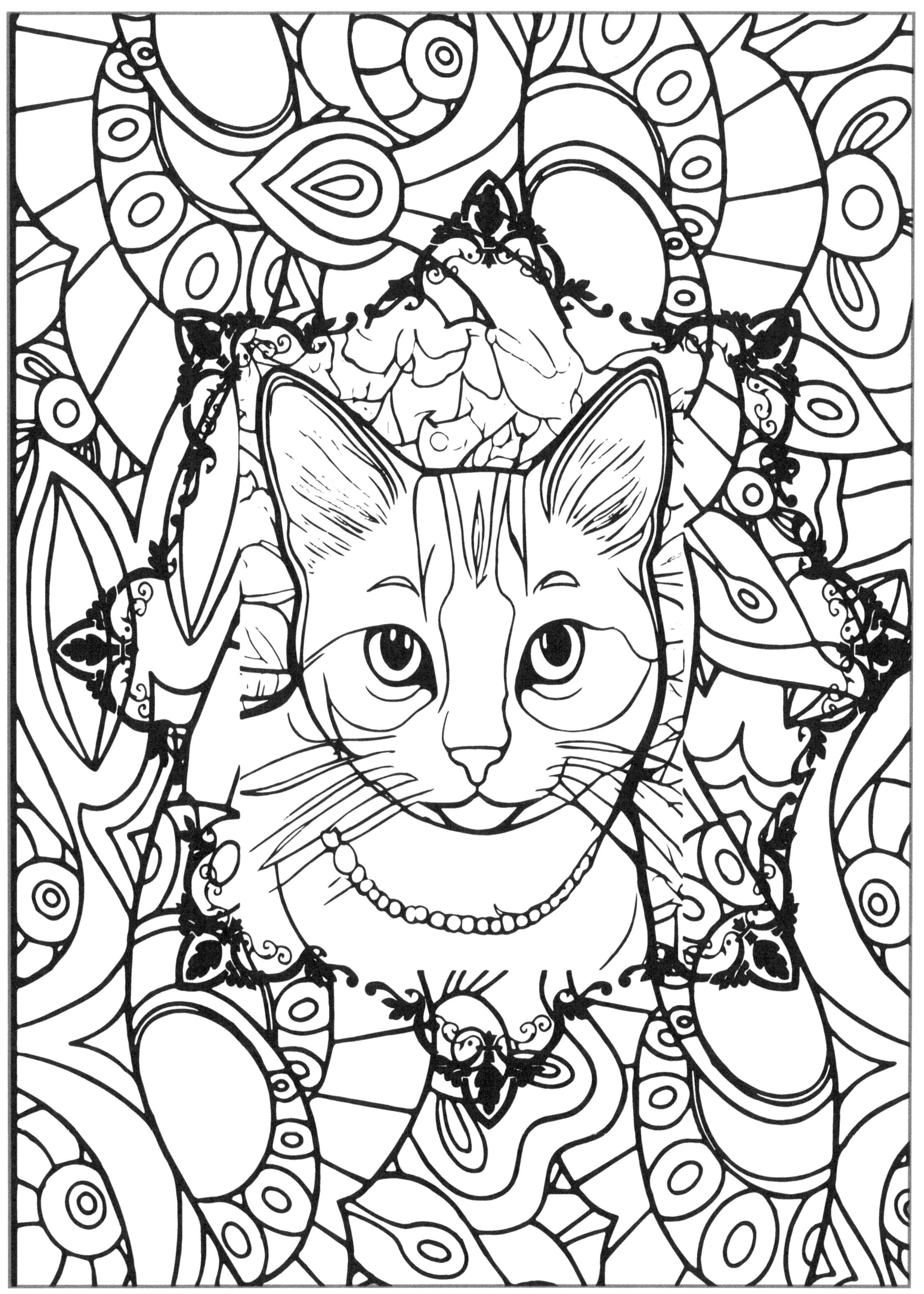

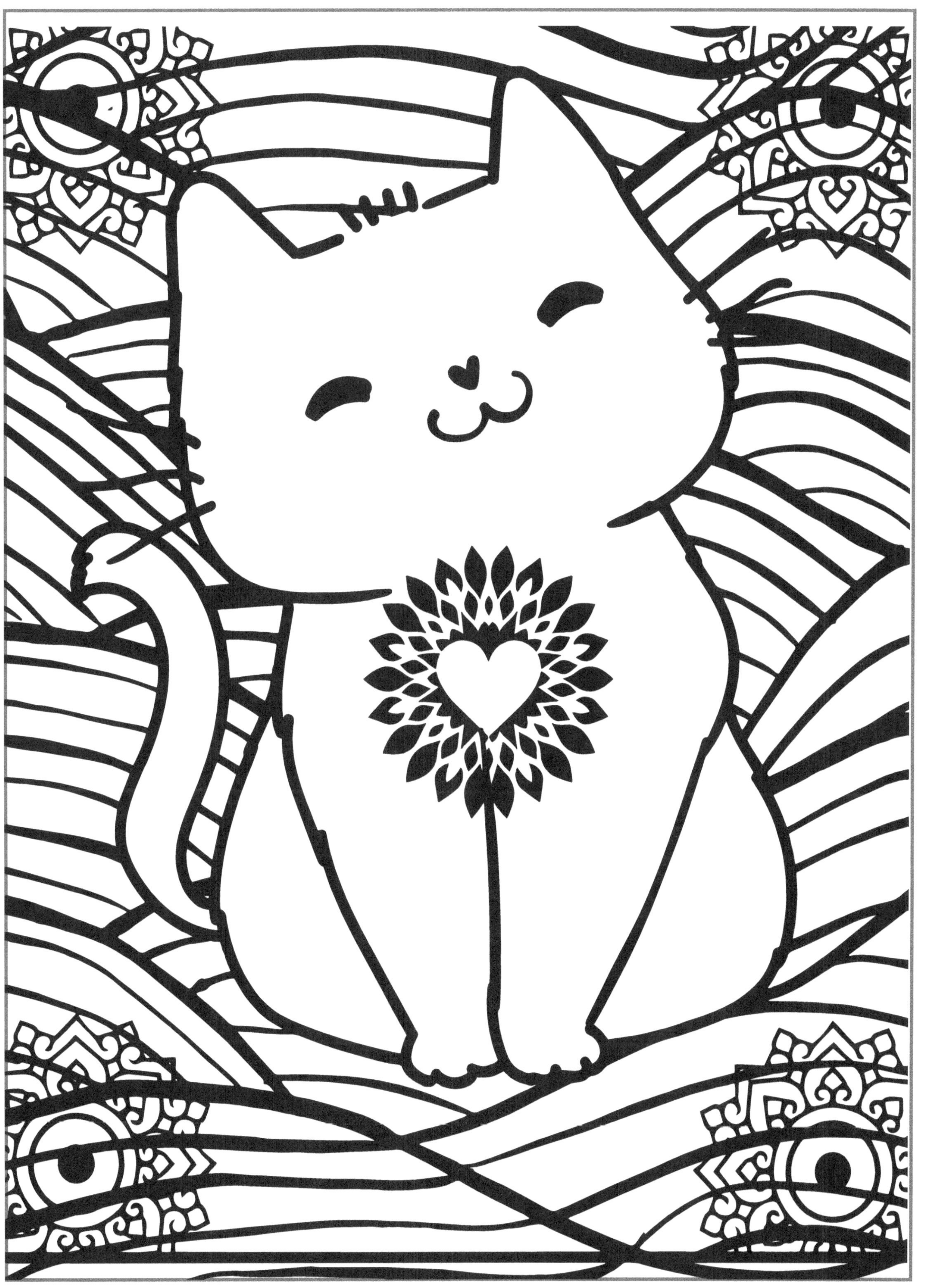

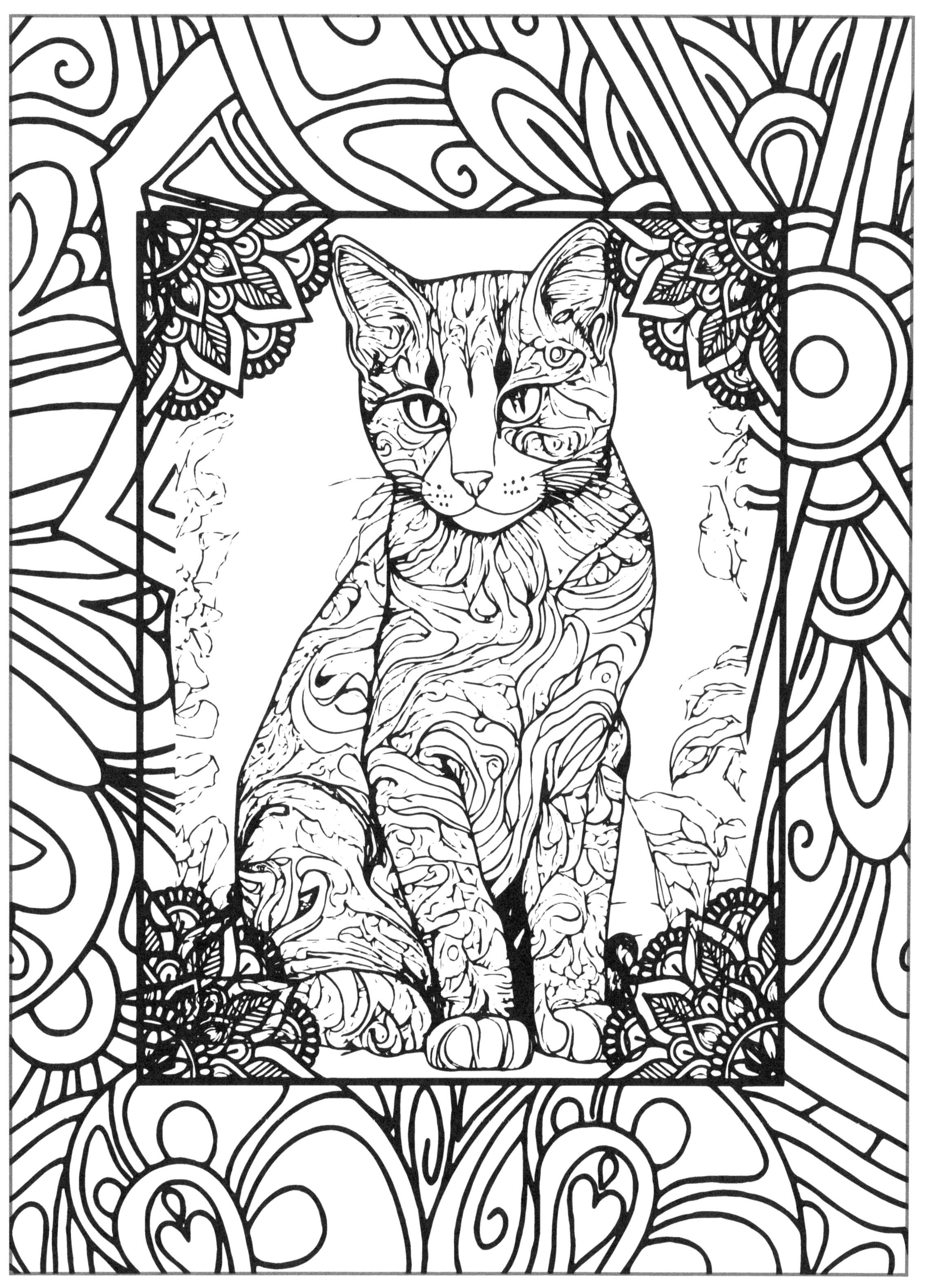

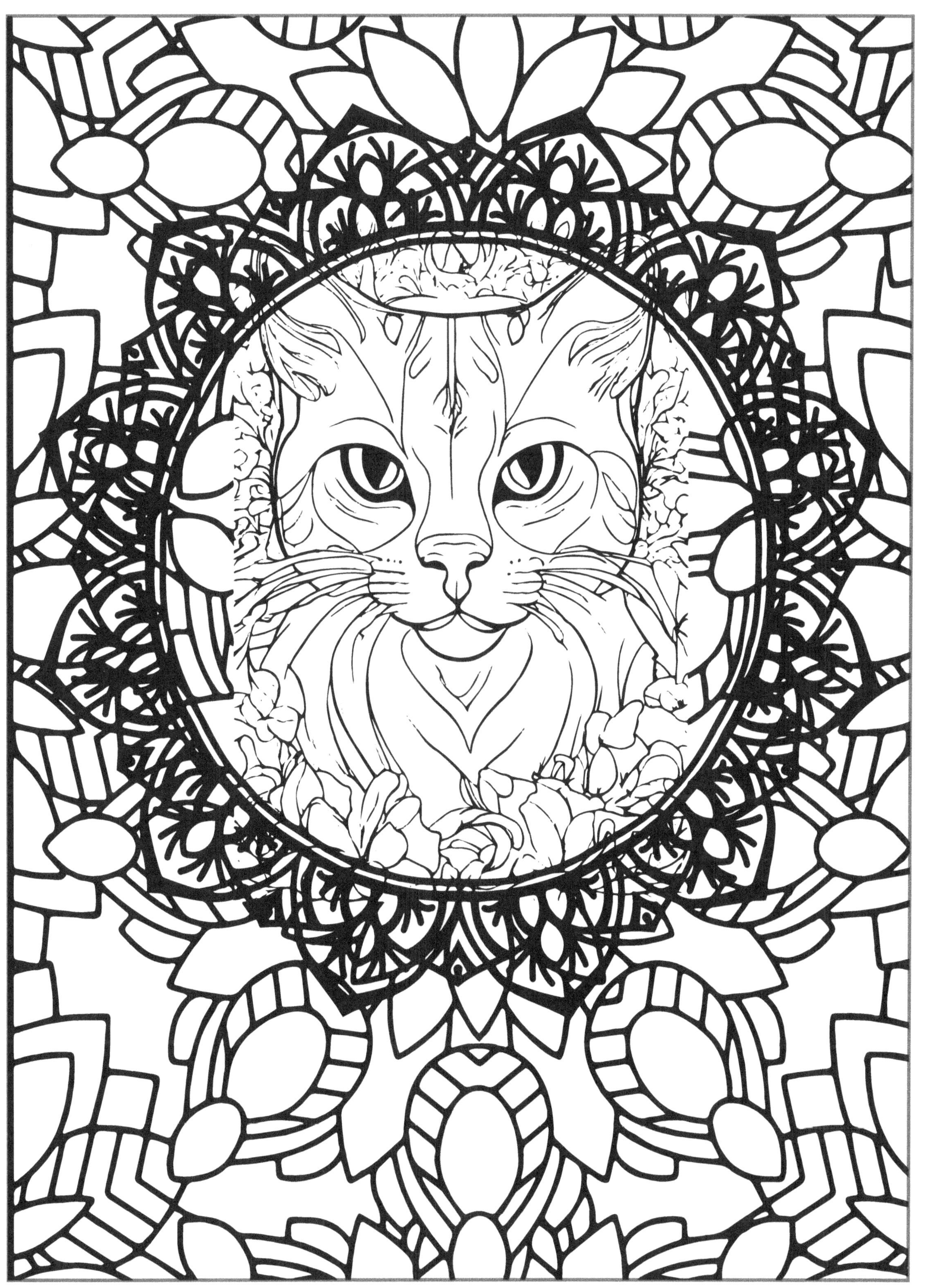

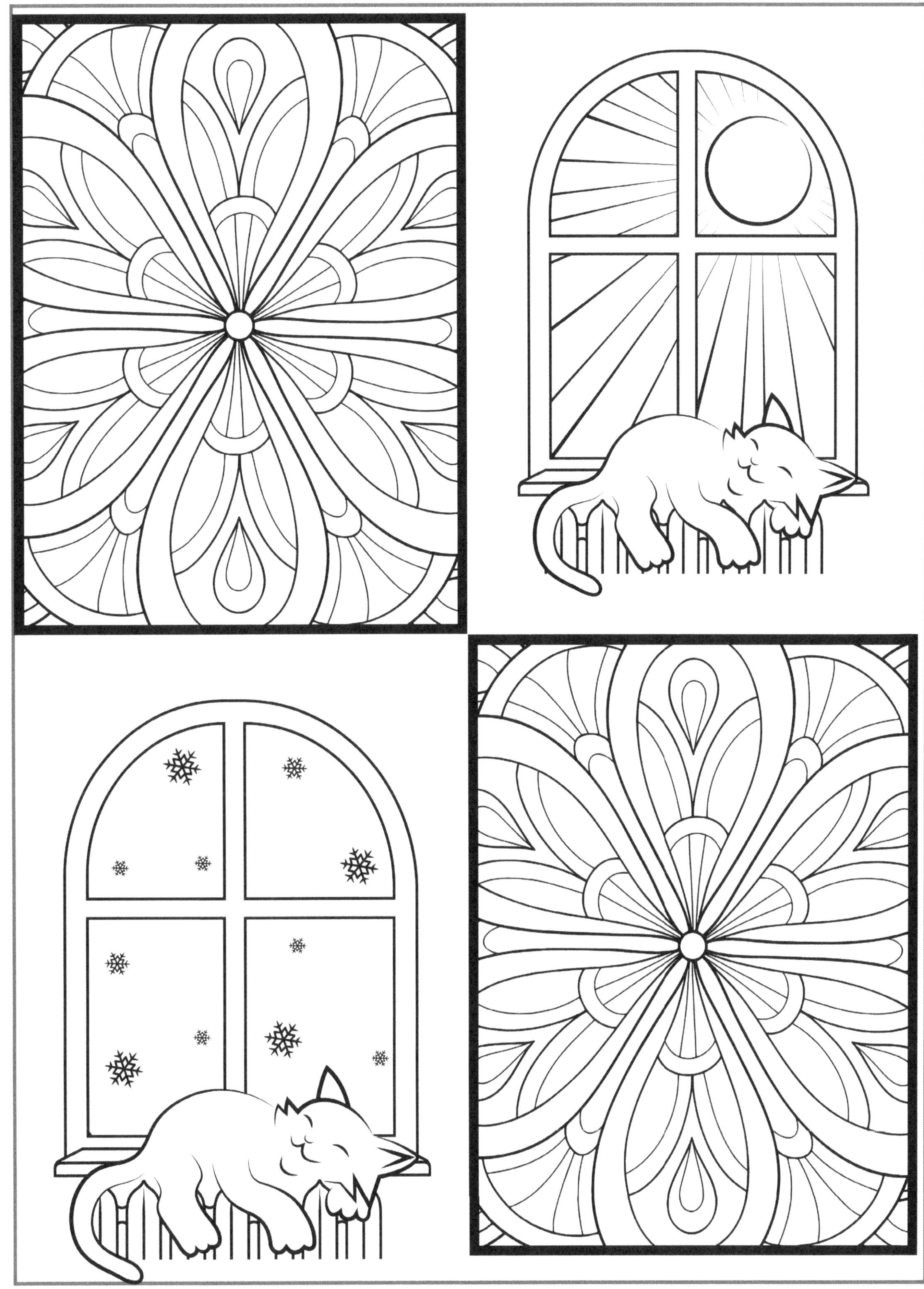

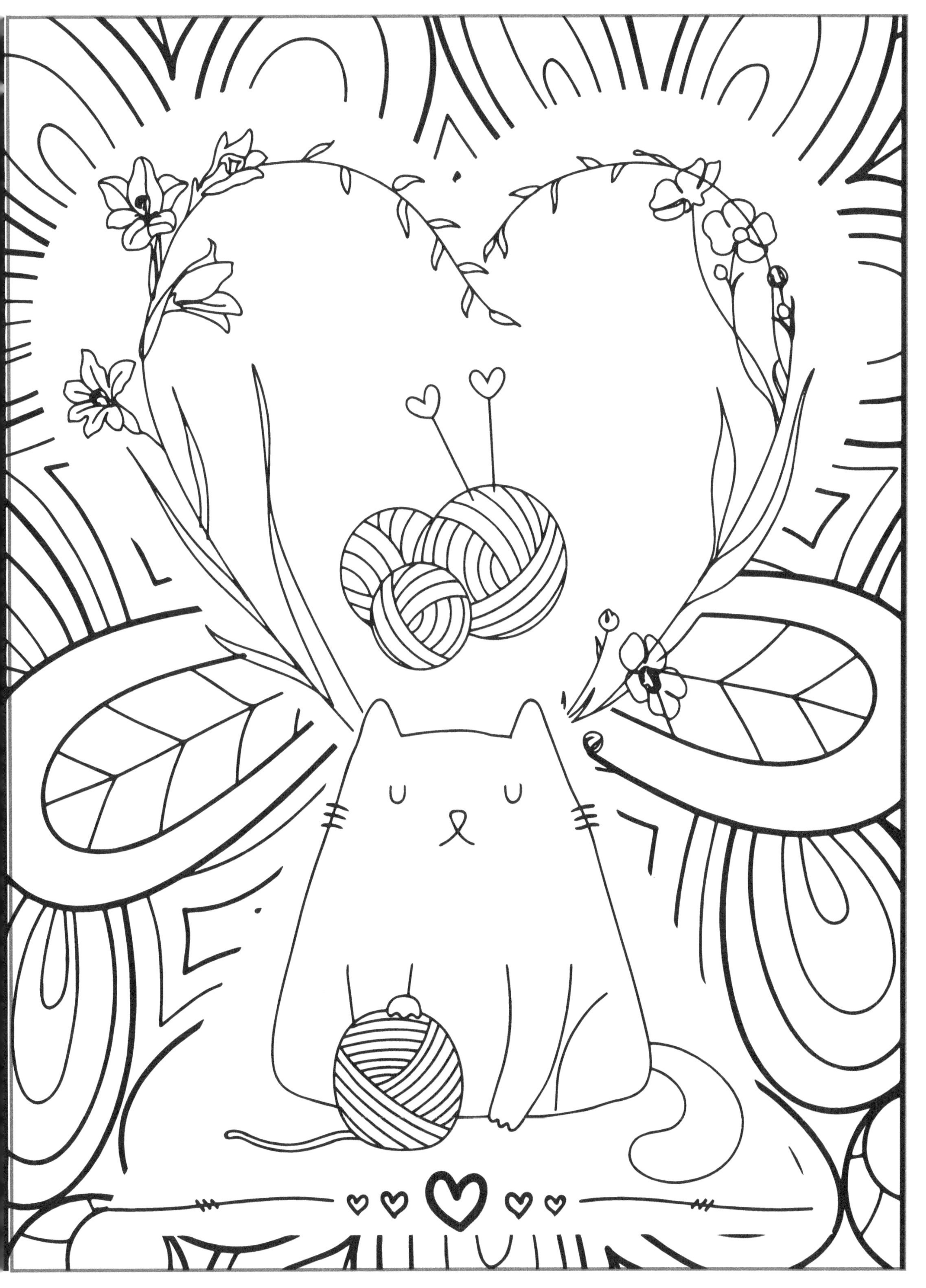

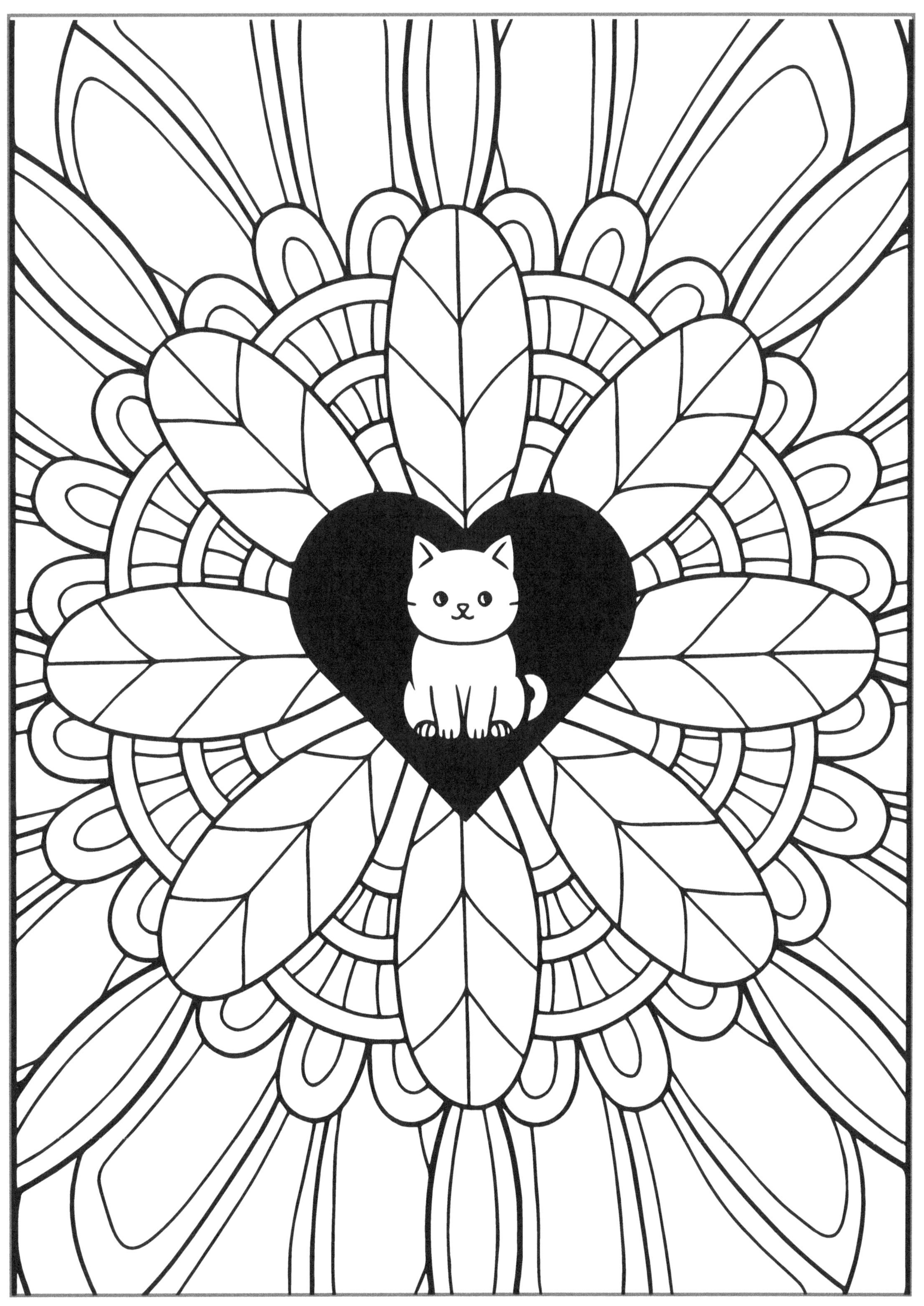

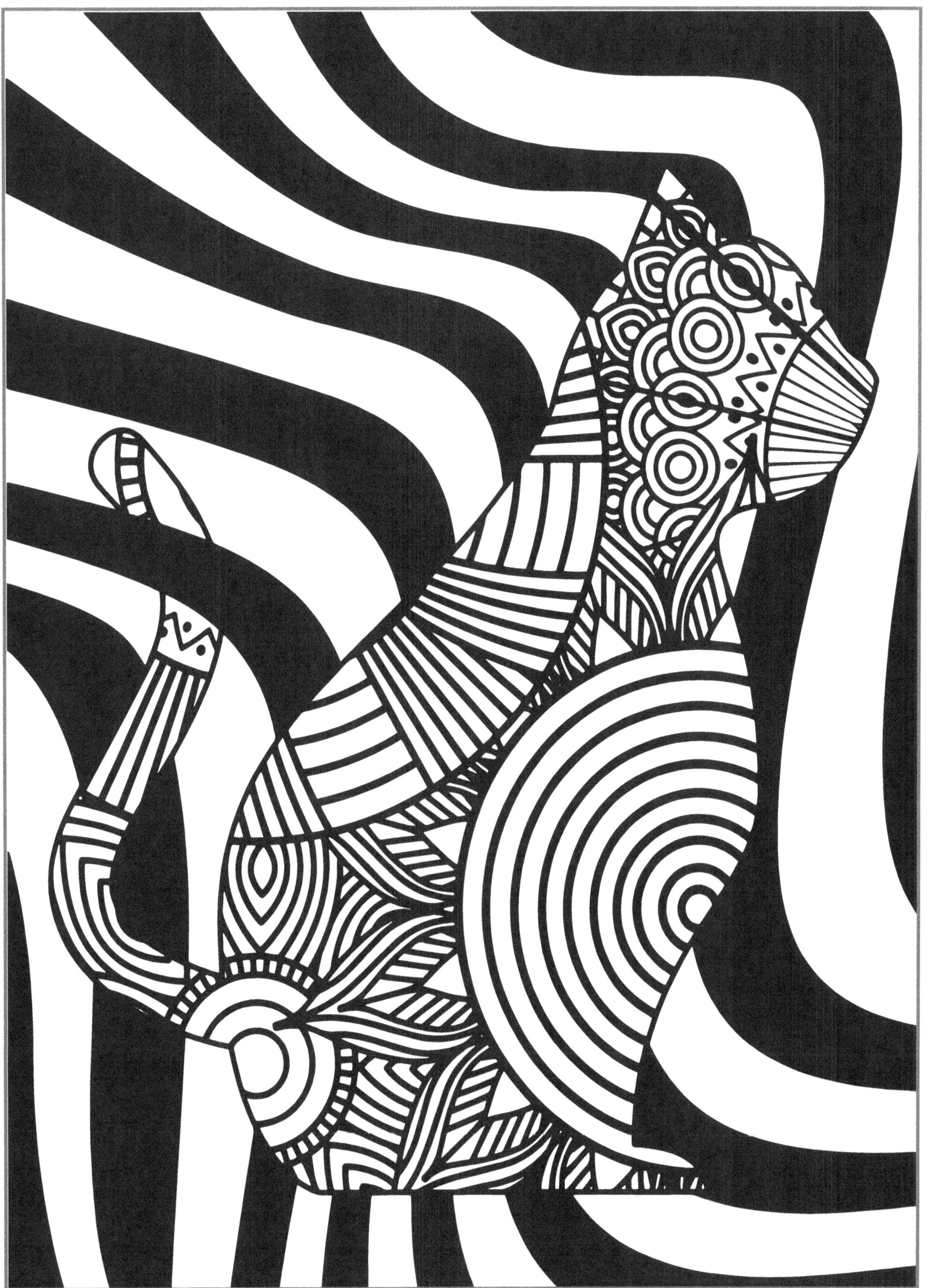

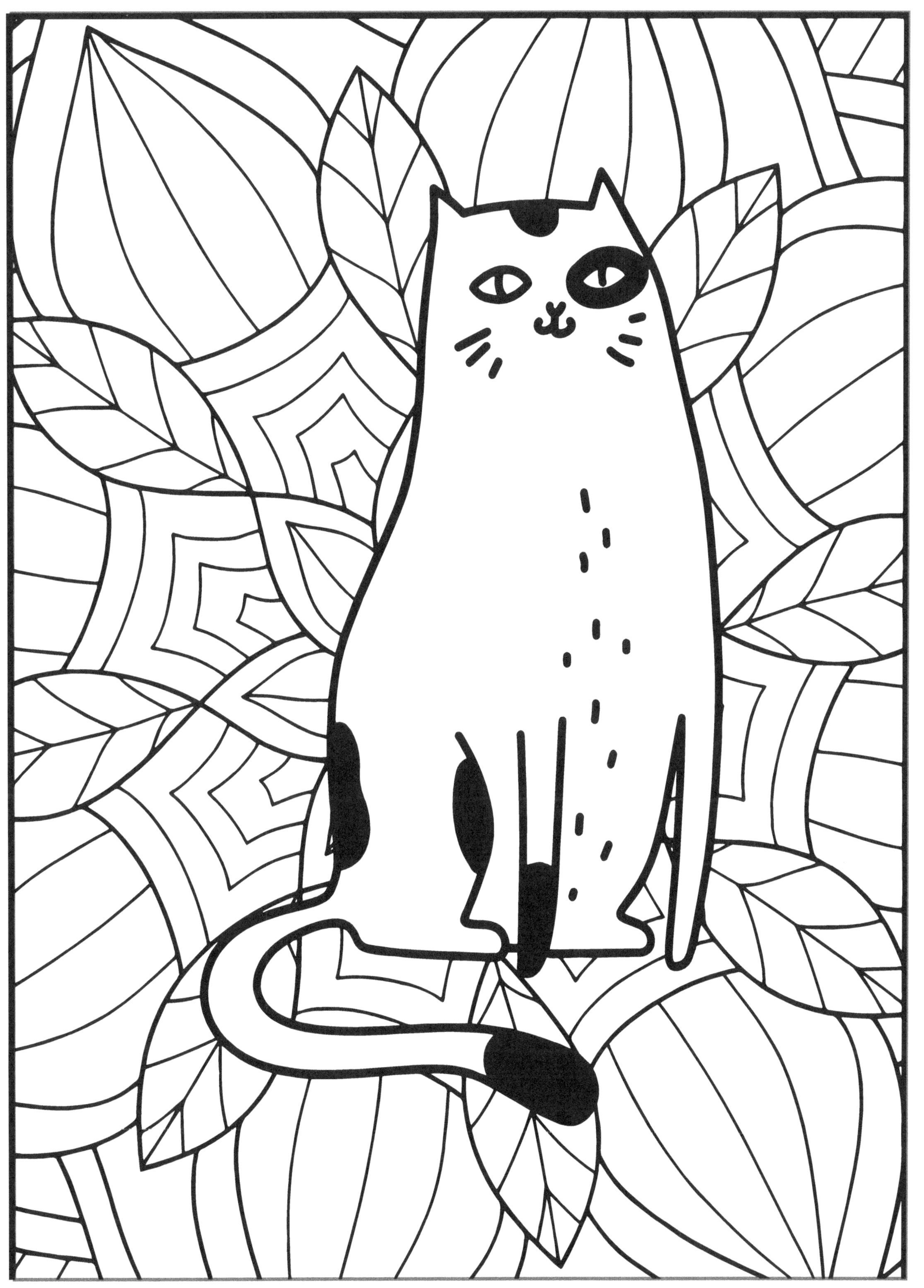

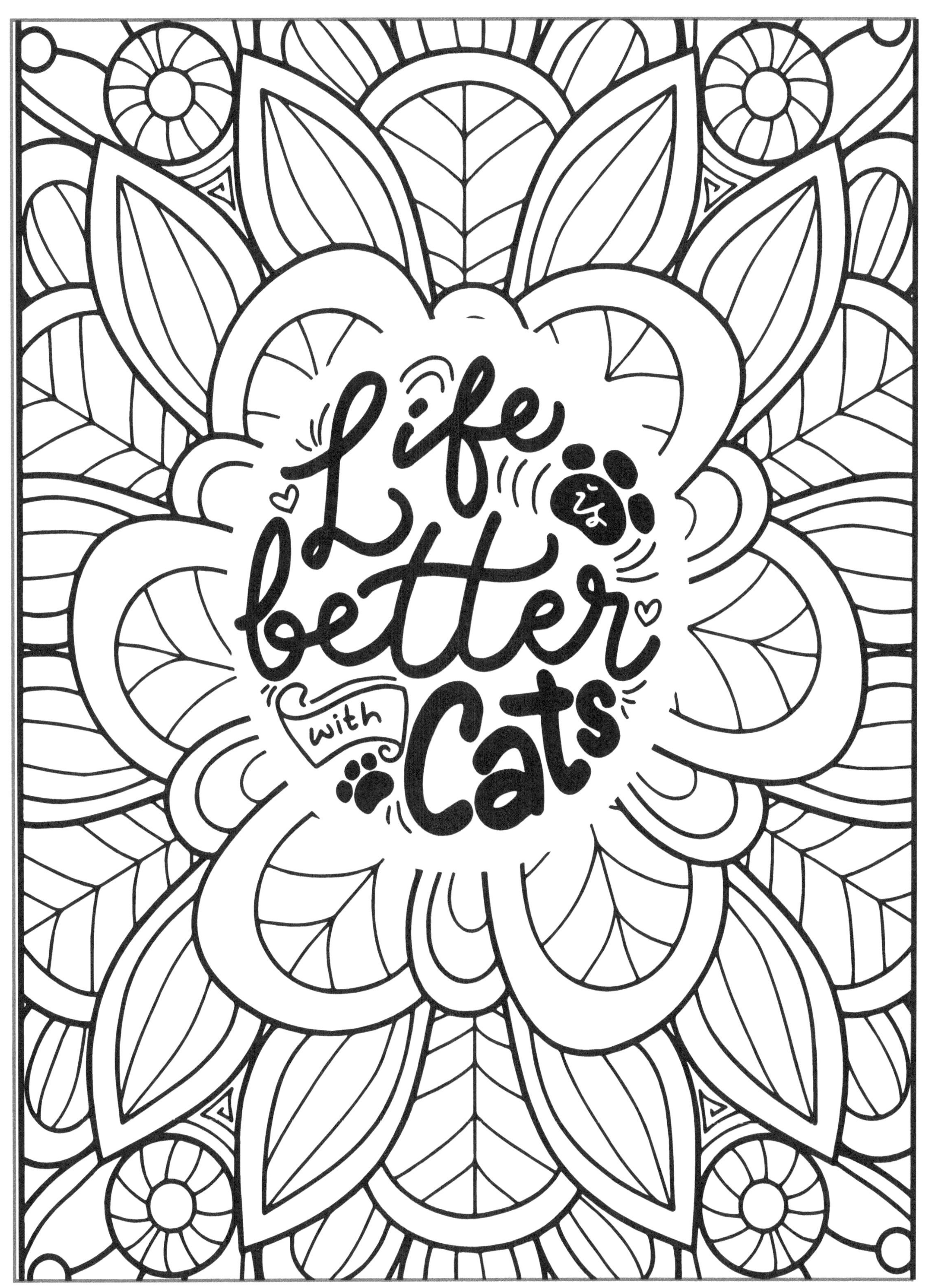

Life
is
better
with
Cats

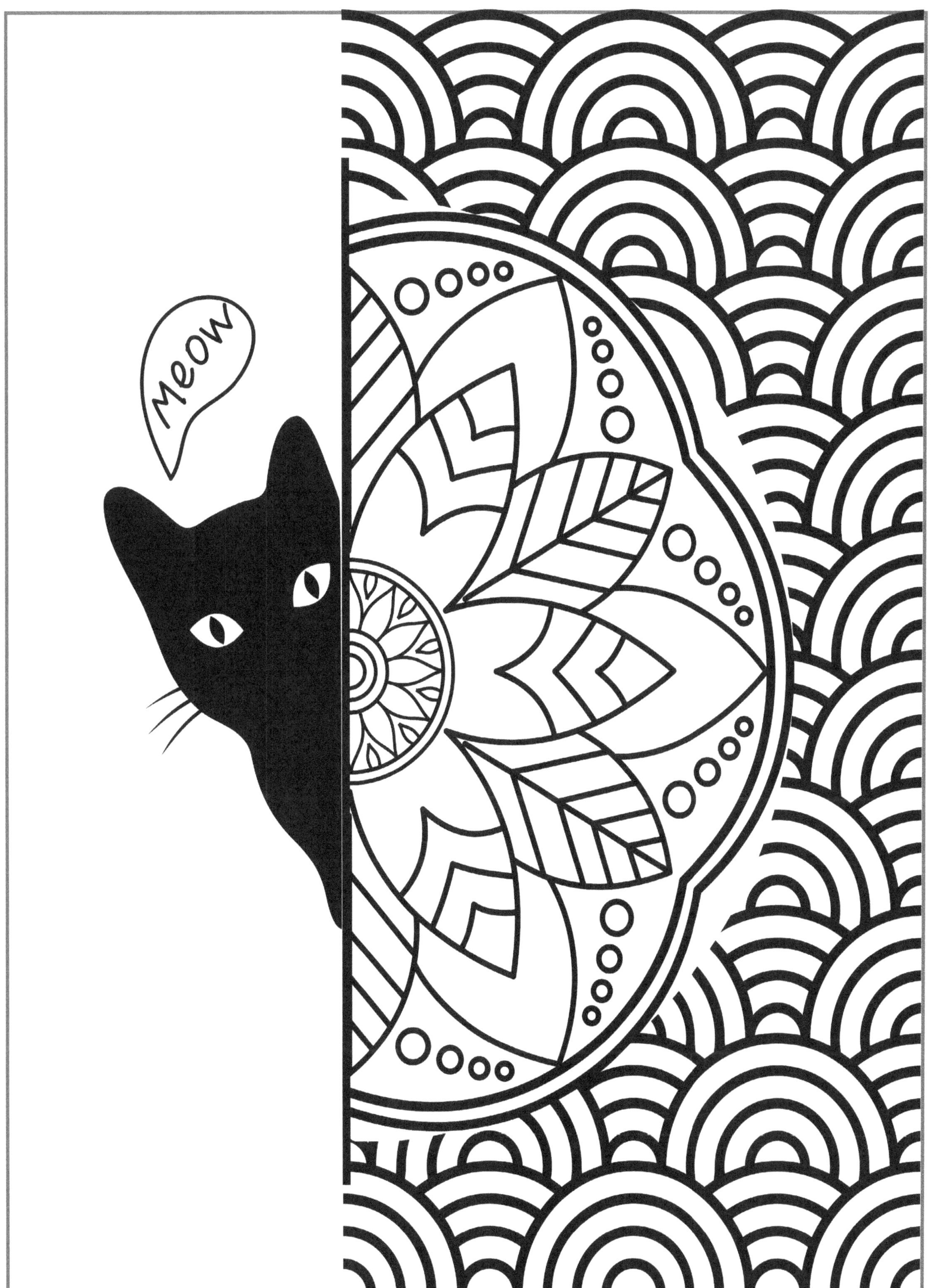
Meow

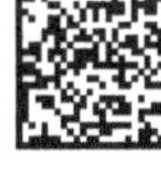